LOVE PROVIDER

A Spiritual Approach To Strengthen Your Marriage

Brian G. Patridge

CONE BREAD
—PUBLISHING—

ALOHA OREGON
TACOMA WASHINGTON

First Edition.

ISBN: 978-0-578-64499-8 (ebook)
ISBN: 978-1-7346114-0-3 (Paperback)
ISBN: 978-1-7346114-1-0 (Paperback B&W)
LCCN: 2020902569

Library of Congress Cataloging-in-Publication Data is available upon request.

Front cover design by Angie Alaya
Stock Photos & Images: Shutterstock
SITH (Self-Identity Through Ho'oponopono) © Copyright 2020 IZI LLC
EC (Environment Changers) © Copyright 2020 Life Discoveries Inc.
Flag Page © 2017 Laugh Your Way America, LLC and © 2020 Life Discoveries Inc.

Cone Bread Publishing LLC
PO Box 6674
Aloha, OR 97007
www.conebreadpublishing.com

For My Love.

A little bit of knowledge

Can be a dangerous thing;

Or it can be a vibrant seed

Giving rise to verdant forests

And awakening sleeping giants.

-Chan Thomas

Table of Contents

Acknowledgments

To God, The Author of Love, and The Holy Spirit, I thank You for fixing this broken vessel, and allowing me to be a scribe and conduit of Love Divine! And how do I begin to thank my phenomenal wife for sticking with me through hell and high-water? Gina, you stepped out of my dreams into my arms; and you've blessed me with the greatest love this side of eternity.

My dearest Jason, David, and Noelle, you know how deeply I love and appreciate each of you. Thank you for all your love, grace, forgiveness, and awesomeness throughout this challenging path. You're the best kids of which a man could ever dream, and I'm proud to be your dad.

My brother Ben, your humble wisdom inspired this book while making it possible. Gina and I are together thanks to all your love and support. No doubt, mom and dad are smiling over us right now! Mr. Larry Bilotta, thank you for showing me how to create an internal environment to help my family heal. Thank you for the coaching opportunities, the years of unwavering support, and for being like a "father" to me.

To Senior Chief Darek Laviolette (US Navy SEAL, Retired) and Pastor Elder A. J. "RightRevRhino" Watkins (US Marines Force Recon, Retired), you both embody everything that "Heaven-sent" and "true heroes" means! The honor of calling you "friends and brothers" is humbling beyond comprehension.

To Mrs. Davis and the late Mr. Davis, this book is dedicated to you. Your overflowing generosity, love, and support means everything to me. You were the vessels through which God delivered my greatest gift in your daughter. To the entire Davis-DeVaul-Patridge-Ferguson clan, everything that I am is because of you! And to my cousin "Bud," you're my inspiration; I'm traversing that bridge in the clouds until we say, with the last breath we breathe, "Oh what a relief I'm free!"

To every man who chooses to "Keep the 'band' together" and be an "energetic servant" as a Love Provider, "Thank You" on behalf of all Creation!

Thank You All So Much!

To each and every person who contributed to this work, I'd like to say a huge "Thank you and I love you all!" Your talents are all remarkable, and I'm so grateful you shared them with me.

All individuals from Fiverr.com are listed by their Fiverr username (in bold and italics) and their real name (when available) in parenthesis:

Cartoon: Dan "Bizarro" Piraro

Synopsis and Blurbs: *Avamallory*

Stock Photos: Shutterstock

Logo design: *Design15 and akilakasun956*

Cover Design: *pro_ebookcovers* (Angie Alaya)

Illustrations: *moimoi13* (Raymon Mallari)

Illustrations: *nahar22* (Quamrun Nahar Kheya)

Bibliography: *rimbumonica* (Monica Rîmbu)

Editing: *flameshot* (David) *and Vanessa_Holand*

Author Bio and Summary: *Snirz94*

Publishing Consultant: *Katheryn7*

Author Bio: *Authoreva* (Eva Xan)

Index/Typesetting: *Mahamud Hussain Noman*

Beta Readers: Pastor Elder A. J. Watkins, Ben Patridge, *missfrancis* (Stephanie Francis), *Flameshot, Snirz94, Katheryn7, Avamallory*

A Wife's Perspective

My wife Gina is a very humble, "behind-the-scenes," and private person. To honor that, I've focused this book on my personal transformation. This says absolutely nothing about all of the extraordinary work, sacrifice, love, patience, grace, forgiveness, and personal growth that she showed on our behalf. Though she acknowledges the changes in me and the difference it makes for us, she is the true unsung hero in this story. So I'm giving her the stage to begin. In the spirit of helping to transform more marriages, my wife agreed to share the following thoughts in a recent interview about our reconciliation and rebuilding process:

Ever since starting this path, he's been an entirely different person; and it's given our marriage a different spin. In the beginning, a lot of it was letting go of old patterns and old habits that caused us problems. We've been rebuilding, leaving behind our past relationship, and moving forward anew. It has been good, but it has its ups and downs.

It started 50/50 positive vs terrible times, then the positives increased in frequency. I never really thought about leaving again after I saw what he could do and knew he could do it again. I've always said that Brian is truly one of the nicest people I know. He's very kind and has an amazingly genuine heart. And he has never called me a negative name or disrespected me.

He would shut down emotionally, and I would try to tease-out what was wrong. But now I've stopped doing that. In the past, I became very defensive and tried to counter whatever he would say. I've since realized that was Shadow's influence.

I can see in Brian what Shadow is doing, and I can see how he's fighting it. He does it well; and he does not complain. I am so proud and appreciate him for that, because I know that he's doing it to protect me and the kids. I feel special and grateful that he works so hard to not allow that negativity into our world.

I stuck-it-out in the beginning because I was waiting for the guy that I knew was inside to come out again. Now, great times are the rule and bad times are the exception. And the bad times are nowhere near as intense as they used to be...not even close. When he is in a good, open, relaxed place, it means I can get close. When he's not in the best mood, I can still see him, the real him through the mood or scowl. I'm so excited, because I get to be with Brian today, because the real Brian is here. And I get to be my best-self as well.

I admire and respect the work that these men are doing. And it's not for naught. Being your best-self is the most important thing, and that's when true happiness comes. Our happiness is not supposed to come from another person; our happiness is not supposed to come from a restored marriage. But a restored marriage is the benefit of you being your best-self.

I think the work they're doing is amazing. Hopefully their wives get to see that their man is working to be his best-self, rebuild, and create a happy world for himself and those closest to him. And if they can get close enough and connect, they too can experience the benefits of the difference it makes in him.

-Gina Patridge

Preface

The book entitled Love Provider by Brian Patridge is a psychological work that will highly offend you if you are an egotistical person or a narcissist. This literary work will make you face every demon and deep dark secret that you have hidden within the confines of your psyche; that only you and God know about. Mr. Patridge has written a book that will lift you into a realm of spirituality that can only be recognized by someone who has lived in such turmoil and come out of that turmoil better and not bitter.

If you are not ready to admit that you are wrong and correct those wrongs, then I would highly suggest that you prepare your mind to be shaken and awakened to the reality that you may have been living in a fantasy of your own making. For men and women this book is a phenomenal tool that can be used to measure the value, not the cost, but the value of a marriage between a man and a woman. If you cannot see yourselves and the differences between your attitudes towards one another then you are doomed for divorce.

Author Patridge has gone above and beyond through the guidance of the Holy Ghost to bring to us a literary work that will let you know if you are still worthy of being an asset or if you are a liability in the life of someone else. I would highly suggest the chapter entitled "Cleaning Meditation" and its' instructions to make sure that you are correct before you try to correct someone else.

All the Best & God Bless,
A. J. Watkins D. Min. Pastor
SIMONTON GENESIS MINISTRIES INC.

Note To The Reader: Some words and phrases are CAPITALIZED, **bolded**, *italicized*, underlined (OR a ***combination***) for emphasis and effect. Additionally, hyperlinks (<u>blue underlined words</u>) throughout the book will be available on select electronic versions. All referenced sources are listed in the Bibliography.

INTRODUCTION & DISCLAIMERS

Though it's written for men who want to strengthen, repair, or rebuild their marriages, this book is not for everyone. If you're not 100% convinced that you want your wife or family, your challenges multiply exponentially. Why? Already, you must overcome your two relationship histories, your hurt/pain, your wife's hurt/pain, and dark entities dubbed "Shadow" (discussed throughout); also, you must overcome yourself while being pulled in opposite directions. And *you* are *your* most formidable opponent! The situation is further compounded with kids, as they need you now more than ever. If you are certain that you can and will enjoy a successful marriage, regardless of whatever or however long it takes, you've already won! It's no coincidence you're reading this now, because there's a part of you or someone who loves you (that gifted this book) that <u>knows</u> *you have what it takes to be successful*.

Love Provider (LP) is an amalgamation of lessons learned through "trial by fire" in my marriage and coaching others through mending their marriages. It's built upon tremendous research (referenced throughout) and practical application; and it's intended for those who've tried "everything" and are open to a more spiritual approach. That being said, I am nothing special within humanity; and God/Source deserves all credit for anything deemed noteworthy within me. I'm merely a passionate researcher who's discovered a way to help myself and others experience more fulfilling marriages and healthy families. The principles in this book will help anyone with a sincere heart who wants a deeper spiritual connection in their life and/or relationships.

Commitment

Please understand that this journey will take extra effort on your part (okay, maybe **_a lot_** extra, as in my case). When separated or heading for divorce, *I strongly advise against dating others throughout the rebuilding process.* You'll need 100% of your energy focused on you and your family. If you're too fatigued, hopeless, beaten down, or resigned to your "lot in life," you can stop right here. And there's zero judgment. Rest and recharge, then pick it back up when you're ready. But if you're serious about changing your family's destiny and being the hero of *your* story, you're in the right place.

Legal Notes

All outside content included or referenced (quotes, images, videos, links, etc.) is protected under license agreements, permission, or the "Fair Use" provision of copyright law, as it's used only for educational and commentary purposes. There is no affiliation with any individual or organization referenced, cited, or referred other than Life Discoveries Inc. (EC Coach). However, Love Provider is independent of Life Discoveries Inc., the EC program, IZI LLC, and the SITH Basic 1 & 2 classes. I highly recommend you take the classes for yourself.

Nothing contained herein shall be construed as medical, psychiatric, financial, legal, nor religious advice. I am **NOT** your pastor or therapist. Results are individual and never guaranteed. Results are based 100% on *your* efforts.

By reading further, you agree to follow your trusted medical, psychiatric, financial, and/or legal provider's advice, until the provider and confirmed intuition says otherwise. You agree **NOT** to make any changes to medication(s) and/or treatment plans without your doctor's or therapist's consent. Always check with your doctor before starting anything new that can impact your physical or mental health. Marriage, divorce, and separation carry significant legal implications; I encourage you to seek professional legal counsel as soon as possible, if you haven't already done so.

Openness

If you're overly pious, close-minded, squeamish, or easily offended, please understand that I don't pull *any* punches; though, I always love to laugh and have fun. There will be "comic relief" throughout. But we're dealing with the future of your family and legacy, and I take that *very* seriously.

Additionally, I've shown openness, through ample personal examples, to make concepts more relatable and universal. In fact, I'll discuss why the human experience is so *similar* throughout our species.

I am a huge fan of The Matrix, Tron, Star Trek, Star Wars, Inception, etc. I will only apologize once for all the TV/movie references.

Although I quote various sacred texts (including the Bible), Love Provider is intended to be universal, regardless of your faith.

Please know that something I do, say, reference/cite, quote, link to, joke about, or the mere act of my regular respiration WILL LIKELY OFFEND YOU AT SOME POINT. This book is controversial. You've been warned. And with all the love in my heart, I don't really care if you're offended. Why? You do your BEST learning when you're challenged to leave your comfort zone. I am sorry in advance for offending you, as that was not my intention. But "you're welcome" for the resulting personal growth.

I've given you 100% in these pages and I expect nothing less in return. To gain a clear picture of the concepts and principles, you must read through to the end. But take your time. Read slowly and reread to absorb the concepts. Feel free to review the videos and linked materials before, during, or after you read. Some may use this as a "reference book" to look up specific topics. Others may prefer to read it cover-to-cover. You have full control.

~~*

As a hopelessly fallible human, I never purport to have all the answers. By combining my "life's puzzle pieces" with yours, we all gain a clearer picture. But as Morpheus told Neo in The Matrix, "I can only show you the door. You're the one that has to walk through it." And I've lived everything I share.

I wish you abundant blessings and success in this most important endeavor. And I deeply, humbly thank you for reading and choosing to **win** for your family!

Let's get started!

~b

HOW EVOLUTION BEGAN...

A gift isn't a gift until it's given away.

What is a Love Provider (LP)?

The answer is both simple and complex. The *simple* answer is it's exactly what the words say: one who provides love. The complex answer is forthcoming. The challenge is that one must define the two terms to understand fully what it means.

What is Love? *(Good luck getting the 90's song by Haddaway out of your head)*. But seriously, how do we define "Love?" Predominantly, music defines love with boundless romanticism, codependency, objectification, and unhealthy dynamics. Hollywood often portrays love as simplistic, myopic, and lacking in deeper truth or power.

Love is NOT lust, infatuation, or merely an emotion. Love is a choice, a decision, a gift, a conscious attitude, a lifestyle, a perspective, and so much more.

We must dive into various religious and spiritual ideas to discuss love. But after we understand it better, we still have many more questions to answer. How do we best provide it, how often, how much, to whom, under what circumstances, with what restrictions, for what goal/purpose? What result(s) should we expect? What's in it for me? Who, what, and where is the "source" of Love from which we replenish? Do I need to wear pink now? Though the last question is a personal fashion choice, we'll explore the former questions from a scientific, spiritual, philosophical, psychological, biological perspective, and more.

To My Fathers, Brothers, and Sons

In this era of gender redefinition and role-reversal, many of us men find ourselves lost among the pop-culture fray. But to find secure footing in these changing tides, men need not feel emasculated, but use our masculine energy to redefine ourselves, especially in marriage. With their well-deserved and overdue success, women increasingly share or even perform the former masculine role of being a financial "provider." This presents a problem for men because this freedom and opportunity for women doesn't address the innate drive men have to be providers.

Many men feel lost and without purpose as their wives fulfill the woman's roles AND the man's roles. As Dr. Emerson Eggerichs said, "If we were the same, one of us is unnecessary." Instead of shaking our finger at her for "usurping our gender roles" or feeling "emasculated," let's focus on the one thing we, as men, can always provide: Love. It's the ONE THING women need most, which only we can provide, that can never be replaced.

Men are doers, and doers need purpose; and that purpose can be defined as a "Love Provider." Even if we are the sole or main "breadwinner," love is what women need more than anything. Using a bible reference, that's why husbands are commanded to love their wives in Ephesians 5:25, and in verse 33. God knows what women need the most because God made them. God made us too; and men are "DNA hard-wired" to be providers. Though, most men don't know what "love" means to women. We know what it means to us, but we also know that identical words have different meanings for different people (especially women).

We were not taught this. There was no class on this. If you were fortunate enough to have a father who was present, willing, and able to teach you, you're among a very exclusive group. Most of our dads don't know because their dad didn't know, ad infinitum. To compound the issue, movies, music, and media steer us into a toxic culture of negative male images and stereotypes. With a hyper-focus on dysfunction that fuels discontentment, this inevitably leads to divorce.

LP is a perspective shift into an endless supply of Divine Love and safe masculine confidence to stand taller and be a better leader. From this Wellspring, you can show love to your wife, which heals and strengthens your bond. And, along the way, you'll become a "beacon of light" to reconcile ALL your relationships.

Light destroys all darkness, and Shadow is (in my humble opinion) the root cause of nearly all conflict and suffering. To shift perspectives, we must address some deep metaphysical concepts and a few simple ones too.

Heartfelt Love

As obvious as this next statement sounds, it's something we often forget: "you cannot give what you don't have." If you don't understand love <u>and</u> direct some to yourself first, you won't have it to give to your wife and kids. I'm talking about genuine, heartfelt love.

Heartfelt love is the goal and the way. It's a literal statement that means "a visceral feeling of love in your heart-area" that radiates outward in all directions. In other words, use the feeling of warmth and power from your center as your "guiding light" in life.

Before you "eject" from a "woo woo" aversion, consider that spiritual traditions around the world have been teaching this idea for ages. Many faiths teach that God lives in our hearts (or is accessed through the heart). We often search outside ourselves, above ourselves, and sometimes even below ourselves to find a Source of power and influence greater than us. But we're looking in all the wrong places!

Each breath comes from our Creator's Spirit. And our Source is literally, figuratively, metaphorically, biologically, emotionally, spiritually, and mentally <u>inside of us</u>, specifically in our hearts. Thus, when you pray, meditate, or engage in quiet reflection, focus inward instead of outward.

By "love," I'm not talking about the kind found in romance novels, porn, or "chick flicks." I'm talking about compassion, kindness, patience, gratitude, peace, stillness, and all the <u>First Corinthians 13</u> stuff. It's a near-impossible standard that few ever attain, let alone sustain. But if you dedicate yourself to being a "Love Provider," there are unimaginable rewards along the journey. The ONLY way to attain that definition of love is to reconnect with its Source, the Author of Love.

"Then the elements of the sun, called Phoenixes and Chalkydri break into song, therefore every bird flutters with its wings, rejoicing at the giver of light, and they broke into song at the command of the Lord." Second Enoch 15:1. If you've ever witnessed the amazing sights from twilight to sunrise, you can see everything within view coming alive as sunlight bathes the landscape. Next time you're awake at sunrise and hear birds sing, you're hearing a song of praise, celebrating the light of The Creator, which is a physical manifestation of Divine Love.

Regardless if your worldview is spiritual and/or material, we are undeniably designed to live in harmony with our environment. Next time you're in nature, contemplate these ideas. The trees, oceans, skies, lands, and everything that lives within and upon them were created for our benefit and care. We are keepers of "the land" and responsible for creating harmony. We breathe oxygen provided by trees and we're made of water and earth (or "clay"). It all has a common Origin, or "starting-point."

The present moment is where everything happens, literally. The best way to be present and enjoy the moment to its fullest is to embrace life in a state of love. Therefore, the <u>Greatest Commandment</u> says (paraphrased) to "love God with all your heart, soul, and mind; and love your neighbor as yourself." "Yourself" is inherent to that command, and many of us miss that. It's as if God says, "I love you and, of course, you should love yourself and others!"

When you connect with Source and tap into Divine Love, you will instinctively love others. And a Love Provider not only loves his wife and family, he shares warmth and compassion everywhere he goes.

This is not a new message, but it's timeless. And it's an honor to have the opportunity to translate this message for this modern generation.

There are reasons I've been kept alive through decades of near-death experiences and intense suffering. Although I gratefully know (compared to many) I was born with a proverbial "silver spoon" in my mouth, the pain I've felt is a universal human experience. The scripture Psalm 23:4 has a direct, personal meaning to me. I know the "shadow of death" personally and walked through it. In fact, I've been an archetypal "dead-man walking" since a very early age. Here's how:

My Road To Acceptance

As a rambunctious 3-year-old (in Reno, NV), I suffered a severe concussion from doing a back flip off the couch, hitting the corner of our wooden coffee table at the base of my skull/brainstem. Though this injury was potentially fatal, I survived only to be tormented with severe pains, mood disorders, and out-of-body experiences (OBE) whenever I lay on my back. Years later, I found myself depressed and suicidal in high school. With no regard for my life, I drowned my pain in everything-but spirituality, for years.

One night when my parents were out of town, I threw a RAGING house party on Sunday, January 16th, 1994. After cleaning up vomit from the carpet and removing all traces of the party, I went to bed before my parents returned home after midnight. That morning, I was awakened by a bookcase falling on my bed in the 1994

Northridge (California) earthquake. I was protected, as my bed frame stopped the bookcase just short of my legs. But this time, I knew God was trying to get my attention.

After assessing the damage to the house (which suffered a cracked foundation) and realizing that we needed a fresh start, my parents sold the house and we packed-up and left for Austin, Texas. We stayed with relatives while renovating a neglected, roach-infested (yet affordable) old house in the "rough part of town." The night air was sprinkled with sounds of gunfire and the frequent flapping of "ghetto birds." And the days were filled with kind neighbors and BBQ smoke. One evening, an eerie silence fell over the area and dark clouds moved in with haste. It was the "calm-before-the-storm" delivering a tornado that damaged homes on either side of ours. Huddled in the living room, we watched as the funnel cloud skipped over us.

Despite all this evidence for "guardian angels," I still suffered from constant migraine headaches, anxiety, and depression. One day, after another urgent care visit for a migraine, I took a prescription Hydrocodone and my consciousness (InnerMan) floated outside my body. I floated up toward the ceiling, flipped over, and saw myself on the bed with my mom standing next to me. Just as she began to panic because I wasn't moving, I re-entered my body and told her what happened. Though lying on my back contributed to the OBE, I took no more of those pills!

With suicidal ideation since the age of 13, I've wanted to kill myself hundreds, if not thousands of times over the subsequent 30 years. Besides multiple "near-misses" driving home (very irresponsibly) from various parties in high school, I took LSD while camping near the beach and was nearly abducted by aliens (according to the friend who asked them to take me away and my foggy recollection of the "trip"). I've left this dimension three times with DMT and warped space-time with Salvia Divinorum. I've rocked MDMA at raves, huffed lines of coke with alcohol chasers, and smoked enough hash to make Cheech and Chong cough. All of this was a vain attempt to escape my personal hell and find some sort of relief.

The pinnacle was a major auto accident in October 2004, just before my birthday. My wife and I just had another fight. I went for a drive to clear my head and get a snack at a nearby McDonald's around midnight. On the way home on I-5 (at the base of "the grapevine" with no streetlights), I had an abrupt meeting with a stalled car parked sideways on the freeway. With the taillights and headlights perpendicular to me, the car suddenly materialized out of the pitch black road. By the time I saw it, it was too late. After colliding at 60 mph, my car spun around 360°, and was rear-ended by another car 7 seconds behind me going approximately 70 mph.

Thankful to be alive, I forced the driver-side door open, hobbled out of the car, and stood in the middle of the road in a daze. A kind young man came out of nowhere, threw my arm over his shoulder, and helped me to the freeway shoulder saying, "Hey man, let's get you off the road." Once I was seated out of harm's way, he asked if I was okay. In a daze, I looked down the freeway at the oncoming cars and said "yeah... thank you so much for getting me off the road." When I turned back to ask his name, he was gone. To this day, I think he was an angel, likely the same one who protected me during the accident. Or perhaps it was the driver of the stalled car

I hit. Either way, I'll never forget when I looked up at the clear, star-filled sky; everything felt tranquil and right. Minutes earlier, the lack of streetlights nearly extinguished the light of my life; now, the lack of "light pollution" made the stars breathtaking. At that moment, I knew that I was just as connected to those bright heavenly bodies as the ground on which I sat. Police and EMTs arrived minutes later, called my wife, and she showed up what seemed like instantly. Then the ambulance whisked me away, as I lay on the gurney contemplating the meaning of life.

Now, at age 43, I am still alive and on this planet. And I know there is a greater purpose for my life. But I **do not** intend to aggrandize myself in any way; in fact, I've felt like the least of any human most of my life. But there's something inside me that isn't mine, and I'm driven to share it to help others who are suffering. This gift's immeasurable value is in the Divine Source from which it came. But incalculable pain drove me to seek the truth, heal myself, heal my family, and share this with you now. As a wise man once said, "a gift isn't a gift until it's given away."

To prepare to receive this gift, our mental and spiritual perspectives must expand to match this new paradigm. Now, it's your turn! Suspend judgment and read on! Let's start with what inspired me to become a Love Provider.

REDEFINING PERSPECTIVES

Imagine how little we know about our planet, let alone the universe...

Redefining Perspectives

This book was borne out of the blood, sweat, and tears shed along the path of reconciliation and rebuilding my marriage. For over 16 years, I left no stone unturned, seeking anything I could find to improve my marriage. Throughout my journey, I performed an in-depth, multidisciplinary study of biology, psychology, philosophy, religion, anthropology, global spiritual traditions, ancient civilizations, sacred texts, and plant medicines to modern physics, pharmaceuticals, comedy, countless hours of meditation, and more. It was my singular goal to glean as much knowledge as possible to heal my depression and create the marriage of our dreams.

My lovely wife, Gina, and I had an ever-present sense that there was such beauty in each other that shone through just enough to keep us together. After years of separation and a near-divorce, I felt like we were due for some "good years," as we had a marriage made in hell for the first 80% of our relationship.

Before our separation, we rarely enjoyed each other or our family time. There were intense fights and stress, while I struggled with clinical depression; and my family struggled with me. I spent two

(2) separate 3-day stints at a mental hospital and years of trips to the ER for chronic pain (migraines), panic attacks, and suicidal thoughts. We survived financial ruin with a short sale of our home, a foreclosure on a rental home (in which I was a "squatter" during our separation), and a mountain of debt forcing us to file bankruptcy. With our lives in pieces, our marriage buckled under pressure.

Sadly, many of our problems began on our honeymoon cruise where I wanted to jump off the ship. Though unrealistic, I made marriage my "panacea" and was naively shocked when "instant healing" didn't occur after saying "I do." This sparked a debilitating depression that lasted well over a decade into our marriage.

We wed in 2003, separated in 2009, reconciled in 2012, and I moved back in with my wife and kids at the beginning of 2015. Since then, the past four years were some of the best and most challenging we've faced in the rebuilding process.

In 2012, an online course called EC (Environment Changers) provided the missing elements to achieve lasting personal change, enough to prompt my wife to try 'us' again and stick with it. The last part is vital because the road is challenging with lots of rough terrain. But, when your wife believes in you enough to stay as you grow, I can't tell you how much it's worth it! By definition, you can't put a price on priceless. And I've been so thankful every day since we reconciled.

A common crevasse into which we all fall is "victimhood." I've been there. But I would like to offer another perspective that I've found very empowering: conscious creator. We're in-control and always have a choice. I perceive life as an immersive holographic simulation where **we** are the producer, director, editor, and playing the starring role in our own "epic life movie." Source is the Author. As for who manages the Simulation and why, those questions are far above my pay-grade; but this "reality" is likely an interactive holographic movie (or a cosmic MMORPG for my gamers out there) to provide experiential education and entertainment for immortal souls.

And for all those with delusions of debauchery and world domination since "It's all fake anyway," It's true that everyone reaps what they sow in this and/or the next life. Karma has a perfect record in terms of relevance, consistency, and impact. And since we are all connected, **when you hurt others, you're only hurting yourself**.

Sometimes the purpose of a simulation is simply to exist. From the perspective of the characters on a computer screen, the simulation software's purpose is to continue running until the "players" decide they're done "playing." It is analogous to the popular video game "The Sims," but on a much grander, cosmic scale.

Before we entered this Simulation in our "avatars" (dubbed "glove box"), our souls played the part of casting director, wardrobe and makeup artist, special effects coordinator, set designer, and we collaborated with the Author on the storyline and character interactions. This represents the "before-life" as opposed to the "after-life." Similar to the Star Trek "Holodeck," this "life-movie" is a multisensory immersive experience. Therefore, I think that levity and laughter are a mandatory part of this life. We shouldn't take things too seriously, as the feeling of laughter is a brief "sneak preview" of Heaven.

Where does God/Source fit in this equation? That's a huge question, but I'll stick with the Holodeck movie analogy to posit an answer. In this example, God is the Holodeck itself, all the materials and technologies that facilitate it, the Energies that power it, the air, the Starship, the Universe, Void, The Instant of Now, The All, the Creative Spark, Laws of Nature, and Designer of it all and much more. God is the Primary, First and Supreme Consciousness, the Original Author, the Ultimate Intelligence, Source, and the True Power that exists both within **and** outside time. And that's just scratching the surface! As shown in the photo above, God is the sky, the whole iceberg… and the ocean.

Regarding names, I believe they are of the utmost importance with all reverence due. But I also know that one can have multiple names and "titles" in various situations. For example, meet a hypothetical man named "John." "Manager" is his title at work, while "John" is his proper name. To the family, John is "dad," "son," and "husband." To many local middle school students, he's a "volunteer" and "coach." To others, John is "dude, cousin, tenant, tax payer, IT technician, bruh, a**hole (accompanied by another driver's middle finger), author, employee, stranger, creepy guy at the bar, point guard on the basketball court, best friend, worst enemy" and everything in-between. They are all referring to the same person named "John," but represent different aspects or titles.

Similarly, I refer to God interchangeably as "Source" throughout this book for three main reasons:

1. It keeps these intensely spiritual topics universal, practical, and applicable to the widest possible audience
2. It's a reminder of my overflowing gratitude for Everything We Are And Have
3. It's a humbling and empowering non-denominational term for the Origin of Everything

In sum, reality is the "effect" of Source's cause!

We possess a similar power to create with thought and speech, not just energetically, but even physically. We're like kids in "Dad's" house, sitting at His table playing with building blocks and toys He gave us, wearing "clothes" He made for us. That's the difference between our creations and Source's. We "create" from pre-existing materials and processes in the physical realm, while Source created all realms, all particles, processes, motion, and all iterations of Life from them (i.e. you and me).

With all our particle colliders, space travel, chemistry, physics, and high technology, we're always working with the same fundamental set of particles and forces. We have yet to create an entirely new universe or dimension, let alone a brand-new law of physics or fundamental particle. To this day, we're still "discovering" new aspects of reality. Surely, there are realms higher than we've ever imagined, but I'm okay starting with the Source of everything we know.

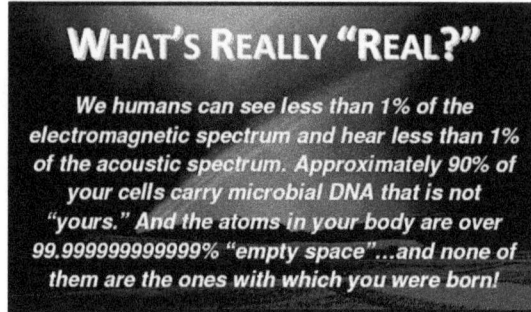

WHAT'S REALLY "REAL?"

We humans can see less than 1% of the electromagnetic spectrum and hear less than 1% of the acoustic spectrum. Approximately 90% of your cells carry microbial DNA that is not "yours." And the atoms in your body are over 99.999999999999% "empty space"...and none of them are the ones with which you were born!

Here's a "quick" little thought experiment: try to fathom creating an entire universe from absolutely nothing, with <u>no</u> instructions or examples. First, you'd likely form a substrate on which everything is built (scaffolding, if you will). Next, you'd invent every particle, element, property, physical and energetic law, interaction/reaction, structure, type and speed of motion, purpose, size/scale, dimension, and fill it all with your consciousness. After creating all visible and invisible objects and life forms, you'd design ways to interconnect everything to manage it from outside AND within, like <u>The Architect</u> and <u>The Oracle</u> in <u>The Matrix</u>. You'd have to design the immense diversity of organisms (from amoeba to animals to aliens), including how they interact.

What's even more mind-blowing is that we base this thought experiment upon our **KNOWN** universe. Imagine how little we know about our planet, let alone the universe and other dimensions. In fact, only 5% of our Earth's seafloor is mapped, as of 2019 (at least, that's what we're told). Human beings have drilled through only half of the Earth's crust; that's less than 0.005% of the distance to the <u>Earth's core</u>. Currently, there's a multi-billion dollar <u>drilling</u> mission that's on track to reach the Earth's mantle

(0.01% to the core) in the next few years. In many ways, we know less about what's under our feet than in the heavens.

The goal is now to fathom the unfathomable. There is an endless variety of things to study in Nature, alone! From Galaxies to grasshoppers and Guardian Angels to gluons, our known universe provides enough variety to appreciate and enjoy for eons!

These stats will change your perspective on many things: http://www.worldometers.info/

Harmony fosters an interdependence that benefits all and allows each to contribute their best.

From our human perspective (seeing life from behind our eyes), everything appears to be "all about us" in our holographic "movies." But that's only half true, depending on your perspective. Our intricate interconnection requires that life can never be all about you **or** all about others; it's all about harmony and cooperation.

We impact the world not only by what we say and do, but by virtue of our mere existence. Consider when a loved one passes away. My older sister died as an infant and changed the course of our entire family in those precious few months. And any child who's lost a parent knows the devastating life-long impacts. This undeniable influence is a form of "causality."

Balance is a positive start that requires **equal** significance, priority, and care on both sides of the scale (AKA "equal weight"). But objects have different weights; thus, it takes different amounts of each to balance the scales.

Harmony fosters an interdependence that benefits all and allows each to contribute their best. Harmony is rooted in mutual respect, empathy, and mutual benefit.

Harmony is to "bartering" as balance is to the fiat money system ("balance" is even a financial term). However, balance isn't enough to motivate people to do or be their best; and we cannot achieve balance while inequity runs rampant. If there are no foreseeable alternatives for balance, the under-balanced side may overcompensate, and chaos ensues. Everyone suffers whenever there's an imbalance (even the seemingly "privileged" or "majority").

Chaos is Shadow's theme park, and he's the owner, manager, and mascot. "Shadow" is a label used to represent darkness, giving it a name and a face. After all, you cannot protect yourself from a nebulous, undefined concept; and the name is a reminder that Shadow is a "person." It removes a lot of the judgment and religious connotations. It's also somewhat non-threatening and something everyone understands in one way or another.

When Shadow is active, people lean towards either of two limiting choices:

The Martyr vs. Narcissist.

And I'm referring to the psychological martyr and narcissist. The martyr corrupts self-sacrifice by riddling it with guilt. Conversely, the narcissist corrupts everything with self-centeredness. This is the essence of polarization and duality. Shadow consistently pulls us towards entropy while Source encourages homeostasis. Thus, we must choose our focus to manifest the desired state-of-being.

In the physical/material world, duality is our default. Yet in the world of emotion, harmony is a defining characteristic of a good relationship. Therefore, it's our job to create it. The instant I shifted my focus to harmony and cooperation, all aspects of my marriage improved substantially.

The best place to begin is from the place of absolute equality. Without equality, harmony and cooperation can be corrupted into slavery and passive-aggressive parasitism. Thus, equality is essential, extending far beyond gender to include race, class, gender, culture, color, status, religion, etc. Let's start by examining how similar we are.

WE ARE THE SAME (almost)...

We are <u>dramatically more similar</u> than different. To understand ourselves and each other better, we often become hyper-focused on differences. To be clear, <u>differences exist</u>, albeit infinitesimal! But in most relationships, your similarities likely brought you together. The question is this: do you focus most on differences or similarities?

Electromagnetic Spectrum

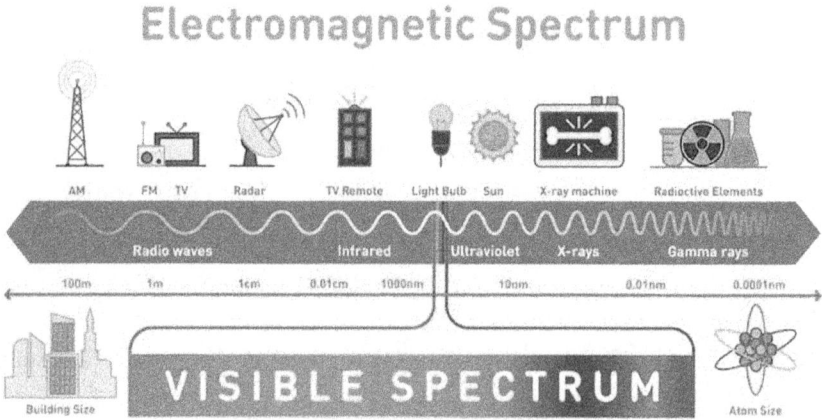

Physically, 99% of the atoms that comprise the human body are only four elements: hydrogen, oxygen, nitrogen, and carbon. Human DNA molecules are 99.9% identical. That means, genetically, we're over 99% similar in terms of race, physical structure, gender, brain structure and functions, biological processes, skin color, age (infants to elderly). Our similarities extend to ancient vs. modern civilizations, cultures, core motivations, "Life Force" (May The 4th Be With You / All Spark), and so much more.

Like diamond facets, most of our differences are merely diverse perspectives of the same thing. Religion, politics, economics, class/caste, education, race, culture, and more are ALL minutiae compared to our similarities. Consider this: how does one measure the value of a soul? Or, how do you decide if one soul is worth more than another? Indeed, humans are over 99% similar in terms of body, soul, and spirit; let's start with that premise.

Consider the immensity of the known Electromagnetic (EM) Spectrum; visible light and audible sound are nothing more than a "blip" on the scale; and they exist at the intersection of ionizing and non-ionizing radiation (ionization impacts matter at the atomic level). Note: the EM spectrum has arrows that extend in both directions, infinitely. The overwhelming majority of our everyday experiences happen within this audio/visual "blip" on the EM spectrum. This suggests that there's a narrow band of experiences many of us share.

Research suggests that emotions are the same for all humans (and animals), though their interpretations differ. If this were not true, empathy would be impossible. Humans are so similar that billions of people around the globe behave similarly under various conditions. And one of the most significant things we share is a common Source and adversary. It is the same adversary of light: darkness (or Shadow and his Empire). Though this adversary has no real power, he can be awfully influential.

Why am I making this point? We've been complicit in our own enslavement by enforcing divide-and-conquer on behalf of our captors (Shadow's Empire). After all, one never tries to escape when unaware of their prison.

Through our ignorance, Shadow continues his divide-and-conquer campaign, until we learn how to cooperate and create harmony. Division is Shadow's #1 strategy, evidenced by global divorce rates, conflicts, and polarization. As magnets either attract or repel, if you infuse negativity into any situation, humans willingly repel each other and create destruction on our slave master's behalf. We're like livestock trained to butcher, package, and deliver each other to the meat market!

Common Adversary

For those who struggle with the concept of "Shadow" and the "invisible world," consider this: few deny the impact of Netflix, YouTube, and social media on all aspects of modern life, yet the Internet is invisible. With Wi-Fi and cellular data, even the connection to the Internet is invisible! Our thoughts and feelings control us, but they're invisible. Unfortunately, this invalidates the cliché, as "ignorance is NOT bliss."

Most humans are a woefully unaware, conquered people with the guise of freedom to keep us under control. We're regarded worse than prisoners by Shadow. He cares for us as much as a weathered butcher cares for his livestock. His concern about the animal's wellbeing is only to protect his sustenance and livelihood. Shadow feeds off our energy and uses us, usually of our own volition, through deception, manipulation, and hypnotic suggestion. The great news is that a common adversary can be a powerful unifying force and catalyst for change.

When light diffuses, photons move farther apart. At a certain point, they no longer enjoy the light amplification effect of neighboring photons, and the brightness fizzles out. Light is destroyed with such ease; divide the photons and darkness conquers the light. Substitute humans for photons, and this illustrates the futility of divisions based on race, culture, status, class, education, colorism, or **any** human's claim to supremacy over another human.

We need to stop fighting each other and team-up to conquer Shadow!

Shadow is one of the least discriminating beings ever created. He'll gorge himself on any human's negative energy with abandon. We're like insects to be exterminated from Shadow's perspective. And to be blunt, the queen, drones, and worker ants face an equal threat from a can of Raid.

We're all subject to the same fundamental challenges because we share a common adversary. This explains why we see the same patterns in relationships across cultures, age, distance, time, background, religion, class/caste, and even gender, etc. Shadow is as universal as shadows cast by obstructed light.

Through hundreds of hours talking with folks from all over the world for the past seven years, I've heard men and women struggling with the same dynamics and pain, over and over. There is no logical explanation other than a common cause and/or influence, AKA Shadow. Marriage is repulsive to Shadow and represents the opposite of everything he stands for.

Is it so far-fetched to consider that we're being watched or influenced by unseen forces? Despite today's surveillance being justified by verbose explanations and flowery justifications, it is still surveillance. When anyone has detailed information about another's habits and thoughts, it's very easy to manipulate and/or control them. Shadow has knowledge of us that is unprecedented, from our words and actions to our very thoughts, memories, and feelings. Shadow is like a mind-reading version of Google, Apple, Facebook, Amazon, Microsoft, the NSA, and all security cameras combined! But unity is the light that destroys shadows and exposes what's hidden.

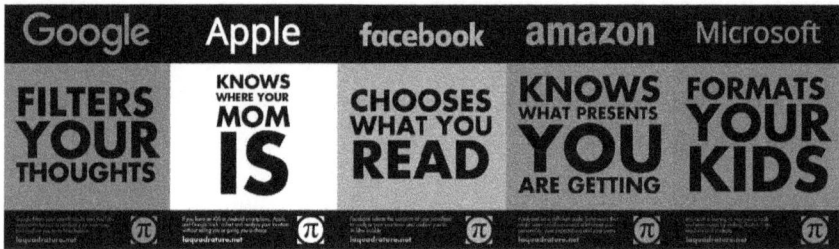

While we're busy analyzing our differences, we're not finding common ground. To have any chance of reconciliation and rebuilding, we must meet our spouses where they are right now. You can't maintain a marriage if you're constantly on higher or lower ground, never meeting on an even playing field. Are you incessantly on lower ground? You need enough self-respect to insist on equality. If you're always on higher ground, humble yourself before the universe does. And size/height is no refuge because "the bigger they are, the harder they fall."

In marriage and all other relationships, let's celebrate how much we're similar, instead of glorifying differences. You'll see strengths and talents in others that you overlooked before (especially your spouse). You'll gain greater respect and empathy, and both are required to work toward common goals. Again, where is your focus, differences or similarities?

Common Ancestry

As a Libra, I'm always seeking balance. I believe-in accommodating as many perspectives as possible to find a truly harmonious state. Modern society's focus on differences has gone from the ultra-minutiae to the obvious. For many years, science has shown and confirmed again and again that all <u>modern humans originate from the same African ancestors</u>. By definition, <u>common ancestry</u> makes ***us all family!***

Instead of division, let's focus on what underpins it all: "The Great Equalizer" or <u>Energy</u>. Energy is everywhere, in infinite quantities and forms. Indeed, the Universe is alive! The most influential energy is, by far, conscious awareness.

Consciousness pervades everything and is equal in all life forms. Thought is equal (though the content and intent are not), just as electricity is the same despite its different forms (from DC batteries to AC copper cables to nerve impulses to lightning). As Bob Proctor once said "...you can cook a man's dinner with electricity; and you can also cook the man." Energy and information, like electricity, is no respecter of men. Anytime you feel superior or think you're better than another life form, you disconnect from your higher-self and everything else. Ask yourself this question:

If Source loves him/her/it just as much as me, why don't I?

Emotions

How do you meet a woman on the same level? First, get in touch with your emotions.

For all those big and tough guys out there, it's time to get "touchy-feely" and focus on those pesky things called "<u>emotions</u>." If emotions are still uncharted territory for you, here's a crash-course:

Begin by observing your emotional state (daily), practice describing your emotions (written and verbal), <u>then</u> apply LP principles to change your emotions. Emotions are fantastic teachers and indicators, especially when paired with intuition.

Having an attuned awareness of your emotions takes time, as does gaining the vocabulary to describe them. One great way to speed the process is to learn from the masters - **women** *(especially your woman)*. Listen to how she talks with you, others, and especially other women. Don't focus on the content because most guys don't understand what they're discussing anyway. Instead, focus on how she's speaking. Take note of nonverbals like her voice inflections, tone, gesticulation, volume, speech rate, eye contact, pupil dilation, and feel the energy coming from her as she speaks.

Women have a rich emotional/feeling vocabulary. By using her vocabulary to describe your emotions, it's easier to achieve mutual understanding. And by tapping into <u>your</u> emotions, you receive the greatest insight into a woman's world. It "automagically" creates common ground and self-awareness.

It's hard enough to connect with someone on the same level, let alone different levels. You do not see things from the same perspective. As a large rope is made of smaller ropes, we are stronger together! We're at our best in <u>unity</u>. Compassion lives here. Empathy breathes here.

Marriage Perspective

Over many decades, trends show that <u>marriage breakdowns</u> are at epidemic proportions. Modern society's focus on "irreconcilable differences" and valuing paper over people (money, contracts, diplomas, etc.) has divided families, impacted countless children, and ruined the lives of a lot of good people.

Let's do the opposite by discussing what we have in-common. This serves multiple purposes: you can better relate to your wife, set a positive example, and work towards similar goals together. Even if she's not yet in the frame-of-mind to work with you, your focus on commonalities will help you both yield faster results. You can expand upon your similarities, for mutual benefit. Turn your stumbling blocks into stepping stones and build a bridge!

Predominantly, Nature operates through cooperation and mutual benefit, <u>not</u> the survival of the fittest. Left to their devices, nearly all life forms in our ecosystem "instinctively develop a natural equilibrium with the surrounding environment, but you humans..." (AAAAAARGH! <u>Agent Smith</u> from The Matrix almost took over!!) I digress.

Natural Selection may be true of genetic changes over time, but cooperation and mutual benefit are Nature's default in a macroscopic and microscopic sense. Flocks of birds, schools of fish, herds of sheep, and numerous microbial colonies are prime examples.

Let's get our "energetic house" in order before trying to help someone else with theirs. Like emergency oxygen masks on airlines, we're reminded each flight to place our mask on first before helping others. How can you help your family if you're a basket case full of "hot mess?"

Your wife is likely to be unmotivated to learn if she's barely holding on for mental and emotional survival. If things are okay and she's open to it, by all means, share! But if you're having relationship issues, the problems become her focus because of all the negative emotions, which makes YOU her focus and the emotional cause of "all" her problems.

For most women, relationships are her world, and failing relationships feel like "the end of her world." But we can take the lead and show her, by example, that learning about the opposite sex has countless benefits. Instead of pointing out her mistakes and trying to help her better understand men, double the benefits by working on YOUR failings and deeply understanding women. Your sincere efforts may inspire her to do the same for you. Men are leaders, and leaders take initiative.

Women evaluate men's words and behavior based on what **they** think and feel. This is true of men as well. Because men and women are so similar, the problem is often translation and interpretation of each other's verbal and non-verbal messages, NOT their intentions. To better understand each other, "Common Needs" gives us insight into each other's perspective. However, non-judgment and an open mind are required.

Common Needs

Just as many <u>flower</u> species need sunlight and water to grow, humans have common needs that help relationships blossom. <u>Larry Rosen's TED talk</u> made the compelling case that basic human motivation is universal. Concordantly, I trust that we share many of the same core needs.

A "need" is something that's required for basic function. Without it, there is dysfunction. Your vehicle needs fuel (gasoline, natural gas, electricity, pedaling, etc.), oils and lubricants, and numerous interrelated parts to perform its basic function. In an automobile, the fuel combines with the engine, transmission, coolant, suspension, emission, electrical, computer, chassis, A/C and heat, light and indicator, wheel/tire, safety, and control systems to move you safely from "here" to "there." Such complexities for such a simple task... yet auto accidents claim <u>thousands of lives</u> around the globe every day. Regardless of driver and design failures, you'll go nowhere or be unsafe and uncomfortable if any vehicular systems fail.

This analogy pertains to relationships in clear ways. If you neglect anyone's needs, you'll go nowhere or repeatedly "crash" on the way. In relationships, needs are non-negotiable and ineligible for use as collateral, rewards, or punishments. Just as we incarcerate those who deprive others of basic needs, needs are things you are responsible to provide for yourself and your wife, kids, friends, family, etc. I don't know what your "life purpose" entails; but this is a "shared purpose" of all life: meeting basic needs. I see all relationships as opportunities to practice fulfilling common needs. In that way, we can hone our skills with others and demonstrate mastery with our families!

Research is extensive on our differences. But information about "common needs" is conspicuously absent from relationship books and websites. For that reason, I'll present my thoughts, based on personal experience, years of coaching others, and a meta-analysis of existing research to find real commonalities.

Below is a list of 9 needs that both partners share in positive intimate relationships. These commonalities promote mutual understanding and a deeper connection:

1. Love   (sustenance & growth)

2. Acceptance   (love & be loved for who we are)

3. Respect   (for self, others, & from others)

4. Desire   (from & for the other)

5. Connection   (compatibility & spirituality)

6. Empathy   (to understand & be understood)

7. Safety   (physical & emotional)

8. Security   (financial & trust)

9. Fulfillment   (individual & relationship)

This list considers the differences between how men and women interpret <u>nuance</u> in words. Though they have similar connotations, "Safety" differs from "Security." To women, safety entails protection from external harm **and** the freedom to be vulnerable. Security is the ability to create what you want, while being authentic, knowing you won't be abandoned. The definitions of Common Needs are self-evident. But it's much more important to define them for you and your partner. This establishes basic relationship health, strength, calm and common ground.

With these 9 Common Needs, it's our job to learn how our partner fulfills them and how to make them compatible with ours. As we all know, conflict and pain flourish when needs are imbalanced. But let me make this crystal clear: <u>no one can **make** anyone feel any particular way</u>. It's ALWAYS each individual's choice of how to respond and what to feel (remember, 100% responsibility). This applies to you, and the same is true of your wife.

This realization can free you from tremendous guilt if she's blamed you for "making her feel" any particular way. Remember, guilt is a counterproductive tell-tale sign of a common Shadow Rx drug in your "bloodstream" ("Freddy Pharmacy" in EC). Conversely, we cannot blame her for our feelings either. WARNING: NEVER share this principle whilst being blamed for her feelings, unless you enjoy the equivalent of throwing gasoline on a bonfire while standing on a pile of dynamite! You must take responsibility for **your** part of the issue and **your** feelings before you expect her to do the same.

By understanding this truth, we can show compassion to the one blaming us for "making them feel" hurt, while not taking it personally. We can focus on healing and preventing injuries instead of being defensive (which helps no one). You have nothing to do with her programming from <u>childhood</u>. The fact that you're a trigger is not your fault. But you can take responsibility to make amends, better understand her, prevent future triggers, and heal the part within you that is connected to the issue. If you dig deep enough, you'll always find the matching energy.

As LP's, it's our job to create an environment conducive to meeting the common needs of everyone (including ourselves), together. Though individuals and couples are unique, this is a good place to start.

Becoming

A client repeatedly asked what words he should say in multiple situations with his wife. After some discussion, my response was: when communicating with your wife, the specific words, phrases, and actions are not as important as your underlying Energy.

Energy is the root. And when you deal with the root, most issues "above-ground" simply go away. If "incompatibilities" or "irreconcilable differences" are considered the top reasons for divorce, I believe there are three major reasons why:

1. They are, in fact, incompatible (chose poorly from the beginning).
2. They were compatible, but grew apart over time.

3. They are just as compatible as anyone else, but haven't learned the skills to cultivate it.

Most believe Option 2 is the biggest reason. But experience has shown that Option 3 is the winner by a landslide. Consequently, you'll bring those energy patterns into your next relationship *until you learn what you need to learn.* The harsh reality is this: if you don't learn these energy skills now, you will recreate the same patterns in subsequent relationships.

Your energy is the "common denominator" in all of your relationship problems. But that's not a judgment, it's <u>The Answer</u>. It means you are the <u>"common denominator" to the solution</u>! Commit to "know thyself," then learn the skills to create a fulfilling marriage.

Nearly everyone gravitates towards where they **<u>feel best</u>**. That's the definition of a pinball, bouncing all over because of their **internal** energy. Most men are concerned with words and behaviors because men are action-oriented. But by focusing on energy, you get to the root of what's happening emotionally (her world). Therefore, the details of "what to do," "what to say," and "how to say it" are not as important as BECOMING the place where she feels best.

ENERGETIC INSIGHTS

If you're a threat to Shadow, you're winning!

Love Provider Principles

Suspend Judgment. Some say, "We are spiritual beings having a physical experience." I say "we are pure awareness having a spiritual experience in a holographic simulation!" The spiritual is mirrored in the physical (holographic), just as our internal subconscious is mirrored in our "external" reality. Remember the axiom, "as above, so below; and as below, so above." You aren't just part of the infinite; you ARE infinite in awareness.

Less than 1% of all identifiable matter is detected using our unaided five major senses. In reality, it's only a fraction of 1%. There's much more to reality than what we perceive. And Einstein said, "One cannot solve problems with the same level of consciousness that created them."

My goal is to expand your consciousness to reveal the powerful being you are. Shadow wants you to think you're powerless and empty (that's him projecting his self-image on you). He propagates the polar opposite of truth and freedom. It's good to know because you can use that to your advantage. Whatever Shadow wants (and his persistence gives it away), create the opposite, intentionally.

Why? Because you can! And like my grandma said, "why not?" To beat Shadow, be MORE persistent with YOUR mental visions than his.

Why do I share so much regarding Shadow? Shadow is the "root cause" of nearly all your relationship issues. That's not putting the onus on Shadow, as we've already assumed 100% responsibility, remember? Though we "allow" Shadow's influence, darkness is NOT our natural state. After we allow him access to our lives, he leaves nothing but destruction and pain in his wake. One of the core tenants of LP is: Shadow's influence is the underlying reason for over 99% of all conflict and suffering. *The key to reconciling and rebuilding your marriage is effective "Shadow management."*

> The shrewdest fraudsters don't sell us fake medicine for real aches and pains. When our ailments persist, the game's up.
>
> The shrewdest fraudsters sell us fake illnesses and imaginary defects. Then the game can endure for a lifetime.
>
> -TheraminTrees

The Shadow Empire needs our energy resources. This means, inherently, Shadow's resources are scarce. If he were self-sufficient, why would he bother with us? Shadow is unlikely to spend resources on you, as an individual, unless you are a threat to him or his agenda. And you may or may not even know why you're a threat. But it's much more efficient to herd us, like cattle, and work on larger groups at once through things like movies/TV, music, all news, mobile devices, internet, satellites, drones, magazines, government, businesses, food (GMO, additives), water (fluoride, chlorine), air (pollution and aerosols), money, medicine, religion, education, hidden alien technologies, etc. I'm NOT saying any of these things are inherently evil. But Shadow can have a substantial influence on them, especially because many of his "agents" operate in the shadows.

Winning

If Shadow is spending resources on you and your family individually, it's because you're messing with his plans. And if you're a threat to Shadow, you are **WINNING**! Remember, we're **not** coming from a place of malice or vindictiveness towards Shadow (as that plays into his hand); we're a threat because our light shines so bright!

You should be concerned only with *"shining as bright as Heavenly possible!"* You need not worry about the myriad of emotions and options before you in life: love is the answer, the guide, the method, the map, the compass, and so much more. Navigate life with love in your heart and watch your life transform!

When you're winning as a Love Provider and things get shaken-up (AKA the "sh*t hits the fan"), **be happy and be encouraged**! Why? Five reasons:

1. It's the last thing Shadow wants or expects.
2. It undermines his efforts.
3. He can't do anything to stop it.
4. You have clear confirmation you're on the right path.
5. You have a clear indicator that a massive blessing is near, and he's trying to distract you from receiving it!

Remember, your wife is the perfect person to help you learn what you need most. She's your spiritual mirror; **so stop blaming "the mirror" for your issues!** If you don't like the hair you see in the mirror, you don't comb the mirror; you style that mop-top on your skull!

In "reality," the mirror (AKA your wife and the "external" world) is merely a reflection of the energies inside of you. Why do we need a spiritual mirror? Most energy is invisible, and most people aren't adept at identifying what's happening inside. The "outside world" does us a service by showing us what's below our awareness. This is the essence of taking 100% responsibility.

In the past, I thought my wife was impossible to please. But **SO WAS I**! Depression, anxiety, and unresolved issues made me impossible to please; but I was so busy focusing on her, I was blind to my gaggle of problems. I was frustrated with the "toothpick" in her eye while a giant sequoia was in mine!

As a wise man once said, "life often delivers your greatest gifts brilliantly disguised as your worst nightmare." Or as an old African proverb says, "The darkest night often heralds the brightest dawn." If not for my personal and marital pain, separation, and near divorce, I may never have met Mr. Larry Bilotta (EC), learned about the Ho'oponopono from Dr. Hew Len's SITH class, experienced true freedom and power, nor written this to share with you now.

I bought into the Shadow distortion that "other people *should* treat me a certain way" which nearly guarantees failure. Why? You're giving up all of your power. You can't control another person, and you wouldn't want that responsibility, if you could.

It's thought experiment time (Another One): Imagine you were personally responsible for every word and action of another human being, within or outside your presence. As the DJ Khaled song goes, "you don't want these problems!"

It is imperative to accept: you cannot control someone else's actions nor guarantee they'll do or say anything in particular. For example, good, moral, law-abiding citizens can inflict senseless violence, loot, and vandalize property while in a mob. Conversely, a mob doesn't guarantee individuals will act any particular way.

We always have a choice. Often, Shadow will attach a partially (or seemingly) true idea to one that gives away all your power. That's the only way he can enslave you. You're infinitely more powerful than Shadow, and he knows it. He has to hypnotize you into thinking you're powerless to drain your life-force safely.

You ARE a good person who's worthy of respect, but others **aren't required** to treat you any particular way to validate that. For example, our ancestors spat on, mocked, and brutally beat Christ Jesus <u>after</u> an unjust trial and <u>before</u> a gruesome crucifixion (talk about adding "insult to injury"). Clearly, One's Identity does little to influence how others treat them.

As Morpheus told Neo during training when Neo doubted himself, "<u>don't think you are, KNOW you are.</u>" *The only one who needs to be convinced you're a good person is you!* Tell that handsome guy in the mirror how much you love and admire him...especially when nobody else will. You are uniquely qualified to comment on you! Stop the insecurities! Stop waiting for others to tell you what **you** can tell yourself (or Source can tell you). You're lovable. You're complete/whole. You're enough! **Know it** down to your bone marrow. Then you'll have the power to influence others or create an environment conducive to a particular result.

Who's At Fault?

We humans must receive some sadistic comfort from believing our problems are "out there" or "someone else's fault." Even if another is to blame, they have long-since moved on, while you're wallowing in self-pity and drinking the "contempt poison" you brewed for them. Plus, it's never beneficial to ruminate on past hurts and/or hurtful thoughts towards others.

Thoughts are things, just as the magnetic field surrounding magnets is real and measurable, despite being invisible. Thoughts have real, tangible impacts on the physical world. It's only when we take 100% responsibility with Divine Love that we're "qualified" to affect wider-scale change in the Simulation.

'IT'S ALL YOUR FAULT ...'

What's the best way to impact all the fish in a lake at once? Affect the lake water in which they swim. Solar flares impact the Earth's electromagnetic field spectacularly (Aurora Borealis) and the Earth's energy impacts its inhabitants (magnetoreception and bird's sight, for example). Furthermore, the solar system's and galaxy's energy impacts us. Since the "external" world is a mirror of the internal, you can create "external" environments through clear mental imagery with corresponding emotions. And that changes the environment from the inside-out. The key is forming pure mental images/movies (holographic, multi-sensory, immersive visions), with corresponding sensations/feelings.

MAGIC ELEMENT: **FEEL IT** AS YOUR CURRENT REALITY, <u>RIGHT NOW</u>, THIS INSTANT; IT HAPPENED ALREADY AND YOU'RE COMING FROM A THANKFUL PLACE FOR WHAT OCCURRED.

Pure movies are formed using clear, concise words. But the emotions are the most important part. After using this technique since 2012, over 90% of my visions manifested in specific detail! I have proof from past journal entries that are now reality. There were many positive extras too. With practice, results became more consistent and continually improved. Now, I believe in miracles which free me to create even more grandiose movies.

Why movies? Images and emotions are the "dialects of the subconscious;" they're the "coding" language of the invisible realm. One thing we know for sure about reality is that it's multidimensional. Why wouldn't the "programming language" of reality be holographic and multidimensional, also?

The next statement is purely my hypothesis: there's a correlation between the holographic nature of reality and the wide-spread popularity of TV, movies, video streaming services, and YouTube. The next level could be tactile holography, and then neural-interfaced immersive experiences. And if we're not careful, reality will cease to be "real."

We develop intuition to "hear" guidance and gain control of our minds. Stillness is the best environment to learn how to "hear" intuition. With practice, you'll be able to recognize Intuition's voice within your daily cacophony of thoughts. That's when things get really strange and a lot of fun!

When you "hear" your inner voice clearly, you can create mental images and speak words prompted by intuition. That's called "pure intention," which eliminates Shadow(s) with your inner light! This state is known as "Living in Inspiration."

Examine your thoughts before taking action on them.

HoloProjector Hijacking

Remember, Shadow is (literally) a mere shadow of your radiance. He's your opposite, your inverse. It's the system "balancing the equation" when you were born, like Agent Smith to Neo in The Matrix. Shadow loves to implant his ideas and images in your mind.

This is important to understand: Shadow is consistent and cannot be anything other than dark and evil. For this reason, we can turn him into an unwilling ally. Whenever he hijacks your mental

HoloProjector to show his movies of your **possible** future, he's disclosing exactly what NOT to do. When you have a mental screenplay of "giving someone a piece of your mind" or berating them, examine your underlying emotions. If it's based on pure love and a desire to benefit them, proceed with grace and non-judgment. If not, keep your mouth shut!

Experience taught me that intentionally "humbling others", "teaching them a lesson", or "getting even" usually results in unnecessary harm. For example, I may PERCEIVE disrespect from my wife during an interaction. My perception could be incorrect, biased, or filtered through my mood, history, etc. Then **I'm** vindictive towards the woman I love for "no good reason," from her perspective. Therefore, she feels unloved while you're still holding a grudge for something that may or may not be true. Lesson: Examine your thoughts before taking action on them. It's better to assume the best, whether or not it's their true intentions. ***An eye for an eye must die***! Allow Source to defend and avenge you.

You can identify Shadow's movies by the emotions they elicit. When he tries to change your movie, smile and say "thanks, but I prefer my version." Then envision the exact opposite of his vision immediately, deliberately. Picture an immersive holographic movie filled with love, kindness, grace, mercy, understanding, gratitude, forgiveness, compassion, etc. As you do, smile as Shadow "pops" like a soap bubble and disperses into thin air! For the best results, follow your movie through to the best conclusion, past Shadow's "suggested" ending.

Use this Shadow tactic for your benefit instead of his: change the ending or meaning of the "movies" playing in your head. Unlike Shadow, when you create movies, **you** determine the ending. That's when you move your awareness forward in-time to savor each moment of <u>your</u> vision's fruition. That is the definition of a win!

Whenever you take control of your conscious awareness, you're in full control.

Perspectives

Shadow looks and acts like you because he's your silhouette opposite a light source. Shadow is neither the light nor the object blocking it; he is only the dark silhouette. Shadows can change sizes and appear different depending on your perspective.

If you were to turn your back to the light and focus on your shadow, you may unintentionally back away from it, <u>closer to the light</u>. This makes your shadow appear larger and more ominous. Then Shadow triggers <u>his</u> choice of your worst, corrupted memories (via hypnotic suggestion). Since you're close to the light, you manifest the negative situation promptly. As you manifest his visions, Shadow uses the light to spotlight <u>your</u> actions (that he prompted) to riddle you with guilt and condemnation.

How Something Appears is Always a Matter of Perspective

But remember 100% responsibility? If Shadow influences you to do or say something destructive, it's still *you* doing or saying it; and **_you_** suffer the consequences, not him. However, 100% responsibility neutralizes Shadow!

Once your back is to the light, his other tactic is to move the surface with the shadow further away. This makes the shadow appear larger. I call this "stagnation." Since the wall is moving relative to you, it feels like you're moving; but you're standing still, as he feeds off your life-force.

There are acts of commission **and** omission that have various results. In other words, you can cause harm both with improper action and inaction. Either option causes negative consequences for you and others. But there's great news; conscious thought is infinitely fast! You can make another choice. You can interrupt the process and interject <u>your</u> movie before his takes hold. Additionally, you can "increase your brightness" and drive-out shadows completely!

Always remember, you're the producer and director of this show. And it takes a simple "pole shift" to face the light again. There's no gradual shift. It's the flip-of-a-switch, on or off, left or right, up or down. The light is <u>always</u> there, yet things appear dark when your back is to it just as clouds hide the sunlight. But you know the sun is still there, right?

In THIS moment, will I choose light or not?

Shadow sabotages your progress by causing you to flip polarity from positive to negative. As you learn more and draw closer to the light, he will try to substitute his fear-based visions to derail you and make you "flip" (pun intended). Indeed, Life can be reduced to a single choice, moment-by-moment: Light or Not.

Ask yourself: In **THIS** moment, will I choose light or not? Whenever you're not feeling well, ask yourself that question to determine where you've allowed Shadow's influence. Be vigilant, like "building a foxhole" on the battlefront to hold your ground and defend <u>your</u> vision. Always keep your guard up <u>as you succeed</u>, knowing Shadow will notice when his favorite meal tries to escape. But you can outrun him with ease!

Shadow wants you to feel guilty about yesterday, fearful of tomorrow, and apathetic in the Present. The last one is the most significant, though. The Instant of Now, the present is the source of **all** power; it's where Source dwells.

The Now moment is infinite and inexhaustible. When Shadow tries to hijack your HoloProjector (AKA brain), substitute YOUR choice instead. And when you do, you must be certain that your vision has the **highest vibration**.

What's the highest vibration?

Love & Compassion

The "LP Litmus Test" for any thought, vision, or idea is how much it reflects love and compassion. Follow your thoughts to conclusion. If they're motivated by love and compassion, you're on track. If not, beware.

When interacting with people, maintain love and compassion by ascribing the best intentions to their words and actions, as often as possible. Even if their intentions are impure, you'll probably never know, anyway. It's an excellent way to be at peace with everyone. Besides, your creative abilities may manifest your positive vision! With that vision, you're "singing a vibrational song" of love and compassion, which has the greatest impact on reality.

The **"best intentions of others"** can always be true in your mind, and that's good enough. Isn't that all that matters, anyway? Perception IS reality. When you approach life from the highest vibration, you'll see miracles increasingly, until the miraculous becomes your new reality.

How does LP help improve your situation? Consider a simple electromagnet: If you send an electric current across a wire surrounding an iron bar, it will create a magnetic North and South Pole. If you reverse the current, the poles flip positions. In terms of relationships, when "the polarity is reversed," you repel people and situations once attracted. In other words, you attract the opposite results. This goes both ways. Wherever there's matching energy perpetuating you and your wife's pain, your love and compassion can "reverse the current" and reconnect you both with your higher-selves, instantly. One day, your energy pushes her away; the next day, your energy draws her in.

Time

And why couldn't it happen instantly? <u>Time</u> is an <u>illusion</u> anyway, right? Think of it this way: a YouTube video exists as a data file on a storage array somewhere on the Internet (or collocated in multiple "somewheres").

The video is a complete story, from beginning to end. It's predetermined, yet dynamic and malleable from within (for all you "Predestinationists" out there). All timelines, options, and possibilities exist; but you navigate them through a choice of your free will.

In this metaphor, the "YouTube video data file" is in a state of quantum superposition (implying *the past, present, and future are malleable*). All possibilities exist, navigated by choice, like those adventure books where you choose your character's path. Or like

"Bandersnatch" on Netflix, where all endings exist for the movie, but we experience different versions based on our choices along the way.

But to experience the full video and unfolding story, we must infuse time. Without time, everything happens "Now," but nothing happens, like a standing wave or static data file. In the YouTube example, Source is to our "reality" as we are to the YouTube file. Since we're outside the data, its internal time doesn't impact our dimension (i.e. fast-forwarding and pausing the video <u>does not</u> impact our reality). Thus, time is malleable, in terms of perception and perspective (hence the saying "time flies when you're having fun" or feeling like something "takes forever"). Even Einstein's <u>Theory of Relativity</u> describes the malleability of time.

But faster isn't always better; especially with certain activities... pleasurable, satisfying activities... shared with your wife... like a delicious meal... hey, get your mind out of the gutter)! Like a candle-lit dinner with soft music, you set the atmosphere. You are the warmth and glow that illuminates your awareness and those around you. Light gives diamonds their sparkle. Otherwise, they're merely cold, sharp pebbles in the dark.

Time is an illusion from the perspective of Source. Since we're operating in higher dimensions as Love Providers, we can embody calm with certainty in everything. If you knew all of your needs were met by Source, would you ever be in a hurry? Breathe. Smile. Time is both of the essence <u>and</u> utterly irrelevant, simultaneously.

Love vs. Fear

It's widely accepted that love is the highest vibration; fear is the lowest. They are polar opposites. In contrast, hate is slightly closer to love than fear on the "spectrum of emotions." Hate is a powerful expression of what one thinks of another. Hate requires that you care about its object, on some level. If one truly doesn't care about another, they'll be apathetic but incapable of hate. Since hate contains an element of care, it can be redirected to love easier than fear.

Love draws things in; fear drives things away. Hate drives things away and creates destruction. But Dr. Emoto's water experiments showed that <u>neglect is the most destructive of all</u>. And neglect is often fueled by fear; while love, compassion, and gratitude are tied for 1st place as the most beneficial!

We shape reality by combining pure movies with strong emotion: love or fear. This explains how Shadow can use you to create all manner of suffering through fear. Your heart and mind form the vision, and emotion powers it into reality.

Besides neglect, the most destructive energy is "repellant or against energy." This energy repels because it's based on fear. And a clear image of impending doom elicits the same physiological "<u>fight-or-flight</u>" response as when you're in mortal danger. Fight-or-flight is the definition of "against energy." "Against energy" is like flipping polarities on a magnet to repel instead of attract. In that state, you create all of the things you fear most. That explains why <u>you become what you are against</u>.

While you're down, Shadow drains your energy for sustenance, then uses you to inflict more suffering on others to line-up his next meal. In the spiritual realm outside the proverbial "glove box," everything exists in vibrations (like "Fluidic Space"). Therefore, Shadow must manipulate us to produce low vibrations for his benefit.

That's why it's all about love. It's NOT because of some flower-power hippy sh*t (though there's nothing wrong with that, all you judgmental hypocrites), it's because Love is the truth and the answer. Why reinvent the wheel spiritually? If nearly all major world religions and countless other disciplines venerate love, I think we have a consensus.

Shadow has no real power other than what we give him, **literally**. He has conditioned people to believe everything is separate. Why? It's the classic divide-and-conquer tactic again. Shadow wants to separate you from Source, others, and imprison you within your body.

We are the beings within the body, not the body itself.

The body is like a "glove box" for our soul/spirit (used interchangeably) within this dimension. The glove box (AKA the Flesh) is theoretically where the "sinful nature" lives. If so, the being inside the body (our soul/spirit) can be cleansed and reborn. This is all within the context of loving all reality, including oneself.

We must treat our biological vessels ("cell suits" or "glove box") with the same love and respect as everything else "out there."

Everything is connected, but we've been deceived to believe otherwise. Shadow uses fear, anger, anxiety, depression, hopelessness, self-loathing, and many other low vibrations to make you generate the energy he needs to live. We can generate those vibrations, in abundance, in numerous situations. But it all starts with what's happening within us.

From adolescence to my late 30s, I had horrendous body image issues. I hated multiple things about my body that embarrassed me for decades. During a particularly deep meditation, I considered my body as an independent, living being. While contemplating the relationship between my spirit, body, and Source, the reality hit: this amazing Handmade vessel (body) in which I experience reality has been subject to unimaginable hate and disgust.

Others hated my body based on skin color and various other physical differences from my peers. Perhaps they were jealous of all this sexiness (in my mind, at least)! Internally, I hated my body for garnering so much disdain. I believed the lies and internalized them. It broke my heart to think of what I've put my body through. I used the Cleaning Meditation on myself for months (and I still do). I've had to learn to respect my body (Diamond Rule) as the blessed gift that it is.

~~*

A single water droplet appears separate, small, and isolated. But pour it into the ocean, and it becomes the ocean. What is reality if the brain is merely a receiver and processor of holographic data? I'm not sure, but simulation theory makes the most sense to me. Einstein said, "Reality is an illusion, albeit a persistent one." Meditate often on the idea that "it's all an illusion." Mahatma Gandhi once said, "Today is the tomorrow you worried about yesterday. Was it worth it?"

Today comprises the present, past, and future. But which one is really "real?" From the perspective of "today," the future and past exist only in our minds. And the past exists only in the collective memory of those who shared it. The "future" lives in the dreamer's mind (and those who share the dream). If the past and future are an illusion, and we can envision endless possibilities, why not rewrite our past and our future? Hint: The best approach to prevent Shadow's movies is to have YOUR movies already playing. When your mind is full of **your** visions, there's no room for his!

Everything will work out perfectly. All possibilities are always available. But from the human perspective, we have only one chance to live any particular reality. Since we comprise a physical body and an immaterial spirit, we can live within space-time and transcend it. Shadow knows all of this, and he uses corrupt memories and "false futures" to make us neglect the Now. That's how we miss opportunities in our life and relationships. It's also the solution.

Your imagination is the canvas of the invisible realm. Imagine being like Source, flipping through a "Rolodex of realities" and choosing the best ones for each moment. Empowering isn't it? We choose realities based on our inner vibrations (or the type and quality of our emotions) through resonance. Therefore, become the reality in your mind's eye. Feel all of the associated emotions and sensations you can from the 1st Person perspective of experiencing the vision right now.

Embody the experience in your mind and _**feel**_ it in the present. The vision can be of the next moment, a few minutes later, days, weeks or further away; but it must be believable to you. Remember, time is irrelevant in terms of energy. Whenever you think "that will never happen," you create the reality where "that" never happens. Instead, think in terms of "it's already done" or "it's happening now!"

Life Is But A Dream

How does this work? If everything is a hologram or illusion, it can be likened to a dream, as the tune "Row, Row, Row Your Boat" comes to mind. While dreaming, if you believe the dream is real, it controls you. If you know you're dreaming, you control it. This phenomenon is called "lucid dreaming" but applied to your "waking" state. When you know you're in a dream, you can change it, at will (Inception-style).

For our safety and everyone's benefit, we're allowed to make changes to our physical reality commensurate with our level of positive spiritual development. This is a "fail-safe" to protect everyone within the simulation from themselves and each other. As you grow in your love, you're "qualified" to have an even greater impact. This reveals the truth of Shadow. He has no power of any kind. Therefore, he can only manipulate, deceive, corrupt, or redirect **our** powers to achieve his dark goals.

Our bodies are holographic, like everything else in our "reality." Each part of a hologram contains a full representation of the whole. Subatomic particles illustrate this holographic principle. Galaxies and solar systems mirror the structure and behavior of atoms. That means the secrets of the universe are literally within us! This validates "as above, so below; and as below, so above." We won't find the secrets of the universe in "outer space," but in "inner-space."

By definition, holograms are illusions. Besides loving God, family, and all Creation, another important goal is to accept that everything is an illusion. Then you can achieve self-awareness within the dream. We have to clean away all the layers of false programming we've been fed for years. Life isn't all about accruing knowledge and resources to gain power; it's about removing false knowledge that's squandering the resources and power you've had all along. You have EVERYTHING you need, right here at this very moment. And it's available to you at all times.

Either you control your mind, or someone else does.

STILLNESS

Stillness is truth. Stillness is Void. Stillness is power!

Physical matter is Holographic Source energy collapsed via consciousness into a measurable, spinning or vibratory state. Spin = Vibration. Vibration = Illusion. High vibrations impact matter (illusion) directly. But stillness is infinitely more powerful; it represents Void, from which everything came. It's the essence of Now.

Always strive for inner peace/stillness to manifest it around you. It's a gift to your fellow "sparks of life." Just as we keep livestock in fences, Shadow tries to cage our hearts and minds within his illusions. But we're far too powerful to be contained, so he deceives us into believing that we're weak to keep us docile. He deceives us into thinking we cannot escape or the journey is exceedingly treacherous (another lie). The truth is Love Providers make it look easy because IT IS easy. There are challenges along the way, but none worse than the challenges brought about from Shadow's influence. Simply put, Shadow's cage is far more challenging than living in Love's freedom!

Either you control your mind, or someone else does. This is the essence of duality. You're either in-control or out-of-control. There's no middle ground. It's On/Off, Yin/Yang, Positive/Negative,

Love/Fear, and Light/Darkness. But have courage; it's all an illusion. And in stillness, you can see through illusions!

Glove Box Analogy

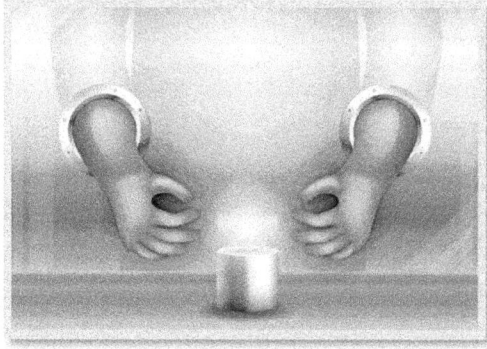

An isolation glove box prevents cross-contamination and allows people to influence something in a sterile environment from the safety of theirs. Within the glove box, both gloves appear separate (as things appear in our reality). But the truth is that one entity **can** control multiple gloves.

This is life when Shadow is in control; he commandeers your "glove box" to control you like a puppet. Shadow pits two (or more) beings against each other or causes individuals to self-destruct, laughing all the way to his dinner table. And your life-force is the main course!

Like a puppet show, <u>when one puppet works independently</u>, it can thwart the other with ease *(Ha! After you watch that last video, that image will pop into your head whenever Shadow tries to create a conflict. Don't laugh out loud or people will think you're crazy).*

Shadow uses us like puppets unless we actively create an internal environment filled with love, compassion, and gratitude. He cannot exist in such an environment. When you embody the light of love, there is no Shadow.

Just as "Vader" in Star Wars is an actor wearing a mask (with yet another voice actor), I like to view Shadow forces as "old friends" wearing masks and using different voices. We all agreed ahead of time that we would help each other grow in our Educational Life Movies.

The moral of the glove box story is this: the "glove" can be controlled by numerous beings, least of which is you. Shadow or other beings of darkness or light can commandeer your body if you allow them. How does this happen? It's no different from you controlling your "glove box." Any further explanation is reserved for the next book.

Remember, there's room enough for the Holy Spirit to take up residence (by invitation only). Shadow cannot commandeer an occupied "home." *In sum, we are the beings within the "gloves," not the "gloves" themselves.*

Internet Analogy

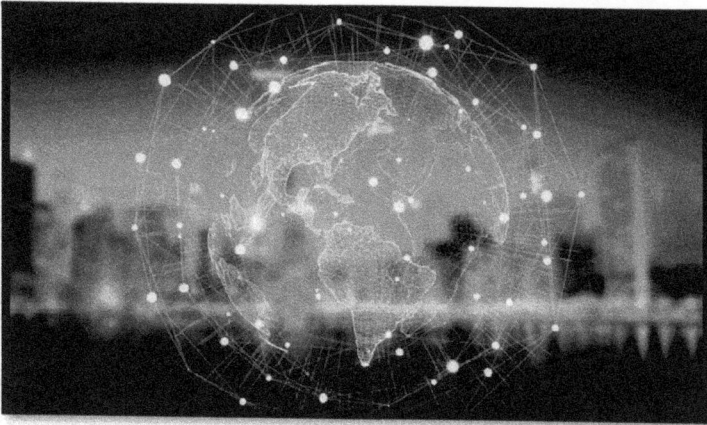

Smartphones tune into specific carrier frequencies called <u>Wi-Fi or cellular data</u> to fetch and send information (through multiple frequency bands) through the Internet. The smartphone is not the entire internet, nor does it access all the information contained therein. The smartphone merely processes, decodes, and presents information on the touchscreen.

Our bodies are like "biological Quantum-Smartphones" that decode specific frequencies into visible light, sounds, physical reality, etc. All human senses are <u>electrical signals interpreted by our brains</u>. Like the Smartphone, our brains do not store the entirety of information available to us; it decodes a "glove box" (AKA body) allowing us to exist and interact within this realm.

Imagine the sheer volume of information that's surrounds us at all times. There are thousands of radio signals, analog TV and UHF signals, satellite radio stations, wireless voice and data, Wi-Fi signals, cosmic rays, neutrinos, and much more present constantly.

And I haven't even mentioned the information density of each strand of DNA!

The information shown on a smartphone appears to come from "nowhere" because it's received through the air. The "Source information broadcast" from the core "holographic quantum computer" (that manages the simulation) exists everywhere, like "Heavenly Wi-Fi." ...as if we're mere software running within the computer. In terms of data <u>and</u> parallel realities, all possibilities and realities exist right now.

Parallel universe theory provides a framework to conceptualize ALL possibilities existing simultaneously. Computer networks have system redundancies to maximize up-time and provide disaster recovery. Parallel realities could be like this. Imagine the trillions of cells that comprise your body (human cells only). If each of your cells represents an entire universe, you can conceptualize how parallel realities could work. If you factor-in the microbiome, parallel universes are a "matter of fact." Indeed, we are made of and express the infinite; and we're surrounded by infinity, at all times.

The vibratory frequency of our reality is far too slow for pure consciousness to exist in its raw form. Can you imagine running a Google search of "cat videos" only to receive a <u>googolplex</u> of search results? Talk about information (and cuteness) overload! With the smartphone example, the interface and software (like your phone hardware, browser, and Google's search algorithm) present the most pertinent information; just as our bodies inform our brains of countless <u>environmental variables</u> every second of every day.

Researchers estimate that the subconscious can process between <u>100 - 400 billion bits per second</u>. Though a large chunk of data comes from our body's internal signals, there's more than enough processing power to <u>observe tremendous information</u> in our surroundings. We only have to remember that infinite information surrounds us at all times, to which we are inextricably linked. And don't get me started on the brain's ability to <u>process</u> and receive information from the future via precognition, remote viewing, etc. Indeed, precognition today equals recollection tomorrow.

~~*

What's the point? When you know the immense power at your disposal, it changes your perspectives and possibilities. It shifts how you see life and puts "problems" in their place. These analogies help illustrate complex theories about the nature of reality and spirituality. This knowledge gives you the power to better resist Shadow's influence, return love for disdain, be patient while feeling attacked or neglected by loved ones, etc. It allows you to shift your thoughts to the Now. Infinite resources, wisdom, and help are available at all times.

These ideas give you better control of your thoughts and your happiness. That is the most important part of any relationship: **to embody genuine love and happiness that's shared freely.** Everyone wants to be with someone who brings forth joy and happiness from an endless supply of love. Be that person!

Shadow is a "Thought Firewall"

On behalf of my fellow IT professionals, the following is an analogy that I've found useful in keeping Shadow's influence at bay: In enterprise computer networks, <u>firewalls</u> are important devices used to prevent unauthorized access to private networks (such as a corporate intranet). Firewalls can be hardware, software-based, or a combination of both. This allows company employees to surf the public internet, while preventing external hackers from accessing the company's private data.

Shadow operates like a poorly configured "firewall" for our minds. He blocks the information we need and allows information we don't need into our holographic BPN (Biological Private Network) and/or our CNS (Central Nervous System).

To limit possibilities, Shadow merely limits access to information about what's possible. And that's exactly what he does in our lives. That's why it's necessary to free your mind! Once I viewed Shadow as a "thought firewall," I could bypass his influence using a secondary "internet" connection with MY firewall in place. My firewall blocks anything resembling Shadow and allows everything Divine. With my firewall in place, I can stop his attempts to infiltrate my BPN/CNS and block his access through love!

Ensemble

Everyone plays their part in the symphony. But Love Providers are virtuosi!

Most of us accept the explanation that innumerable spinning particles form the basis of our physical reality. Atoms are nearly identical other than their speed, position, and the number of common constituents. All Life is similar because it consists of the same subset of particles.

Spin is akin to vibration. Concerning others, vibrations can be in unison, octaves, in harmony, or dissonant. Since we're vibrating beings like everything else, we can harmonize or clash with the vibrations of our environment and others. Therefore, it is helpful to have a framework for harmonious relationships. I've found that music is an excellent metaphor.

But how does this apply to life and marriage? It applies by providing a firm grasp on the nature of reality, so you can influence it! Everyone directs and shapes energies like musicians playing melodies. But it goes much deeper than that. Since one could say music (vibration) underpins reality, it begs the question, Who is "singing?"

The Biblical Genesis story tells that God created everything, except humans, with spoken words. Although humans were "Handmade" by God (Genesis 2:7), our constituents of earth and water (AKA clay) were "spoken" into existence.

Since speech is a form of rudimentary singing, one could say that God/Source "sung" reality into being. Singing is merely speaking with specific tones. And we're made in the image and likeness of Source, right? That would mean we're endowed with "Source-like" attributes and abilities. We each contribute to "The Great Song" by singing particles in and out of existence, moment-by-moment. How do we "sing"? We "sing" via the type and quality of our emotions.

Spoken words are repeatable vibrations, with shared meanings, used to express complex ideas. Since vibrations create illusions within our simulation, we can influence reality with our inner **and** outer voices! Sound creates form. Multiple experiments show this from cymatics to acoustic levitation.

Thoughts and images impact emotions. Emotions impact matter. The vast majority of this energetic "singing" happens subconsciously, by default. We each generate a specific "carrier signal" through our DNA that informs the structure of proteins that form our body. I see DNA as the "tuner" of our unique carrier signal that allows us to "download" our family's data set from the Morphic resonance fields (a brilliant theory by Rupert Sheldrake).

Trees sing their tune, planets sing theirs, and whales sing theirs. Each life-form plays a unique part creating harmony or dissonance with others in "The Great Song of Life." Remember, harmonies and dissonances are both parts of great music.

Driving Home The Point

In this energetic "ensemble," there's zero judgment of individuals playing their instruments. All that matters is the music we're making in the "now" moment. By focusing on the Now and what's just ahead (like reading music or driving), you make your performance easier and reduce burdens, instantly.

The past is less of a consideration while you're present in the "Now" while looking ahead. For example: while driving, you pay the most attention to the road ahead (I hope) and glance briefly at your rearview mirror. By default, you're much less concerned with what's behind or passed along the way.

In life (as with driving), you can only see what's within view. You can use maps, GPS, and other apps to navigate and monitor driving conditions, but your driving experience is based on what's within view. Theoretically, you can make it through the same traffic in more or less time than others based on your ability to monitor conditions and make slight course corrections.

Safe driving is an excellent metaphor for navigating life and achieving success. However, relationships are infinitely more complex because you're dealing with two unique, self-contained trillion-cell symbiotes, with unique histories and perspectives. And yes, we are symbiotic beings. Our skin, our digestive tract, and nearly all our cells (mitochondria) are full of non-human organisms. They outnumber our human cells!

You, me, the cuckoo, and the tree are made of similar cells, save for configuration and a few special structures. But the things that make us distinct have nothing to do with our human cells. It's our microbiome, comprising trillions of bacteria and other organisms! I like to think of them as sentient, high-tech micro-helpers. Some keep our skin healthy. Others help regulate body processes, extract nutrients from food we eat, or provide power for your cells. Many organisms have microbiomes. One could have a microscopic animal living in their body that has its own microbiome. Indeed, we are an Ensemble of Life!

Among our most vital symbiotic relationships is the one with an ancient bacterium called "Mitochondrion." Mitochondria are self-contained, living "power generators" for our cells. They power our bodies! They're individual living entities that facilitate most body processes. But wait, there's more!

Besides bacteria, there are even microscopic animals living on-or-in our bodies on which we depend. As gross as this may seem, what's worse is considering life without them. Some slow the process of decay so our skin doesn't look like an unwrapped mummy. Taken together, this diversity shows that Life is an infinitely complex, interwoven symphony of vibrations.

We are each unique instruments, our families/communities are an instrument section, and we all play in a larger symphony orchestra we call "Earth." Since "the two become one flesh" in marriage, one could use the principles of symbiotic relationships to strengthen their bond!

When anyone suffers, everyone suffers.

Like musicians in a band or studio, all members are equally important and bring their unique talents to bear. Each musician sets aside everything to focus on creating a work of "vibratory art" together, while aligning their intentions to the same moment in time-space. With a shared goal, musicians create something far greater than the sum of its parts, and love every minute of it!

Whenever musicians play together, they build bonds with each other and their listeners. In "The Great Cosmic Song," all instruments are welcome, even the ones considered harsh or "dissonant." Great music <u>includes</u> dissonance and its counterbalance to make it beautiful!

Just as we need each cell we have, the Universe needs you, me, and all reality, equally. The Universe thrives with balance and constantly works to maintain it. That's what men are all about: "balancing the equation" (like "The Architect" in The Matrix movies). Women are all about "unbalancing the equation" (like "the Oracle" in The Matrix movies). But the intention of women **IS NOT** malicious or destructive. It's more like "QA and field testing" our "balancing work." Isn't it wise to test the integrity of a high altitude rope bridge before using it to cross?

Men create balance as a labor of love. Women create more humans through love and intense labor that keeps men rebalancing. In a way, women give men purpose, and vice versa. Men facilitate the creation of new life, which fulfills her purpose. Is there anything more magical than childbirth? Though, men cannot fully relate despite being by their woman's side throughout the morning sickness, cravings, mood swings, and physical discomforts. Even if we are present for the entire labor and delivery process, we have no frame-of-reference for an experience like that. It's uniquely female. Meanwhile, men continue to create balance until the little miracle arrives; then the entire house of cards collapses! But kids are <u>so worth it</u>! They're your legacy.

Though I may or may not know you personally, the blessings we enjoy are clear; in fact, everyone reading this now is blessed with the finances, time, access, technology, and mental/physical abilities to read these words. Consider those without the same access and abilities. Consider the disabled, homeless, hungry, ill and/or incarcerated. Consider those who eat thanks to an EBT card, or those living one paycheck away from losing everything (I've been there in both cases). Consider having to feed your family through donations from food banks, Churches, and/or panhandling. Remember, we're all over 99.9% similar.

As Martin Luther King Jr. said, "injustice anywhere is a threat to justice everywhere." Simply put, when anyone suffers, everyone suffers. Like a musical ensemble playing together, the entire group sounds "off" when one musician is "out of tune." Consider the human body. When one part of a limb (like a toe, knee, shoulder, back, neck) or organ is impaired, the whole body suffers and compensates. The body reallocates resources to best serve the needs of the whole. This is another example of the truth: if you change one part of a system, you change the entire system.

Instead of judging someone who's already suffering, give them a hand-up instead of a hand-out. The difference is tantamount to "giving a man a fish" vs "teaching a man how to fish," respectively. However, when a man is hungry, please give him a fish to eat before trying to teach him anything!

We MUST stop judging our homeless brothers and sisters. They're NOT all strung out on drugs, lazy, or "freeloaders." Do you want to know who they are? They're your mothers and fathers, sisters and brothers, daughters and sons. And don't think you're too far from the same fate. Everyone who lives paycheck-to-paycheck is only 1-2 PAYCHECKS AWAY FROM BEING HOMELESS! Even if someone is hooked on illicit drugs (understandable given the hell of homelessness), **DRUG ADDICTION IS AN ILLNESS**! Like mental illness, it must be viewed and treated as a medical condition instead of a "flaw in character" or some other judgmental opinion.

Keep "The Band" Together!

Compassion is one of our greatest strengths as men. I'm not talking about a "soft" emotion here. Compassion is rooted in connectedness. Compassion can engender "tough love" to immeasurable grace. Compassion means "resonance with the vibratory experience of another." It's based on empathy, NOT sympathy. What's the difference? Empathy fosters connection; sympathy does not. It's looking at life from behind someone else's eyes to *see* (sympathy) and *feel* (empathy) their unique perspective. Even if we have only a brief moment to spend with someone, a smile and encouraging word (and some practical help) doesn't take long; and it could make their day. We can all relate to marriage and family challenges. For that reason, let's encourage and build each other up (and ourselves along the way).

Every member of the Ensemble is valuable and necessary. Just think, what's your favorite song without an instrument, the melody, or harmonies? It's incomplete. As I've learned through 25+ years as a professional musician, you can never fully replace another musician in an ensemble. You could put the identical musical instrument in ten different musician's hands, and you'll hear ten different sounds and styles, even with the same selection. You may find someone who melds with your group and knows the music, but each musician brings a uniqueness that cannot be duplicated. **The same is true of your wife!** And if you have kids together, you're connected for the rest of your (and your kid's) natural life! She is worth the commitment, work, and investment in your family's legacy.

The Ensemble needs everyone to play their part. Keep the "band" together!

Knee-Jerk Reaction... minus the knee

We, as a society, have adopted a new modus operandi for things that need repairs, summarized in the phrase: "Throw it away and get a new one." I call this the "Jerk Reaction."

This approach may work for computer components, car parts, home repairs, even certain body parts; but this _does not_ apply to marriage. When dating, the "Jerk Reaction" is normal because you're still "playing the field." But when you make a marriage commitment, it's no longer a viable option to throw your spouse away. People are NOT disposable!

Relationships are based on commitment and trust. Relationships foster personal growth. One cannot experience growth if they run away from their problems. Imagine if a plant ran away from the heat of the sun. Soon, the lack of sunlight would make it wither and die. If your default reaction is to "escape" every time you have conflict, you are **not** mature enough for marriage, at all. And if you're already married, it's time to catch up real quick.

I understand the desire to quit in the face of colossal challenges. All winners experience it, but they push through to become champions!

To quit on a relationship is not a "free" option either! You've invested tremendous time, energy, and resources in each other. If

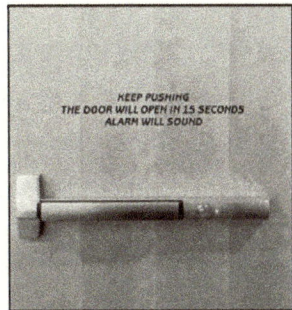

you walk away, you <u>both</u> stand to lose a lot. Children multiply losses by **at least** 300X per child.

In terms of commitment and investing in your relationship, we all know, "do as I say, not as I do" **doesn't** work with kids. Kids emulate what they see, hear, and feel from you. You cannot expect them to have strong, secure marriages after the example you set.

Stay, don't run away! Your children pay the price in their relationships, impacting future generations. After a divorce, you may rebuild and regain a lot; but "simply" walking away can cost more than you can fathom. To say the loss is "devastating" is an incalculable understatement.

We're treating our lives like individual sprints instead of a "team marathon relay" race. Instead of thinking about yourself and how <u>you</u> feel, think about what you want for your kids, your great-grandchildren, and beyond! Set the plan in-motion immediately!

And I have great news: marriage and family investments are **not** subject to fluctuations in the market. And, <u>you can influence returns DIRECTLY!</u> Compassion, forgiveness, repentance, grace, gratitude, and love significantly increase your chance of success.

Spiritual Covenants

Early in my EC studies, Larry Bilotta explained the difference between a spiritual covenant and a commitment. As most of us know, a commitment is a social contract that is broken constantly.

However, a spiritual covenant is a special contract where you declare what you will do, regardless of what the other party does.

Why? A covenant is between you and a higher power regarding another being. On our wedding day, many of us promise a higher power that we'll love and care for our partner for life. In marriage, it means loving your wife whether or not she reciprocates. It's the closest we can get to "unconditional love." Of course, she reciprocates often, but my actions are <u>not</u> contingent upon hers. It's very empowering and negates the transactional dynamic.

Therefore, invest in your relationship instead of throwing it away. When you achieve something significant, despite the odds, it makes for some of the greatest stories ever told. Be the hero of your story; don't be a jerk! Don't give up when you're at the threshold of a breakthrough!

You got knocked down? So what? Learn from it, get up, train harder, and guard your chin next time! Like all the greatest who ever achieved success, dust yourself off, and go at it again! Resist the "Knee-Jerk reaction" to take the easy path and give up. Embody positive masculinity and declare that "the buck stops here" regarding your legacy.

When light is absent, the "consciousness of darkness" is no longer held at bay.

We Are an Intersection

We are a dynamic, multidimensional intersection of electromagnetic (EM) Source Energy. Our cells have a <u>vortex of EM energy rotating within and around them</u>. Your body is a conscious creation in the physical realm. We've learned recently that electric current propagates via the EM field surrounding the wire. With the iron in our blood, our blood's motion and the numerous crystal structures throughout the human body generate electricity and bio-photons.

During gestation, <u>the heart is the first organ to form in the developing fetus</u>. <u>The heart holds memories</u>. In our "cell-suit" (or body), the heart is our TRUE <u>CPU</u>, not the brain. <u>Many indigenous people teach this from a very early age</u>.

Each heartbeat is an energy rotation (or cycle). Everything happens in cycles, from our 365.256 day trip around the sun to our roughly 24-hour sleep-wake cycle (circadian rhythm). Life follows a larger cycle of birth, growth, and decay. In the same way, our heartbeat corresponds to the spin of fundamental particles as perceived within the instant of Now.

We're the result of the interaction between two spinning spheres of Source energy (synthesis of masculine and feminine energy). As each collocated energy sphere spins, it creates a separate expression of consciousness that is "you." In other words, the two spinning "energy spheres" create a 3rd independent rotational axis (as a Father and Mother beget a Child). That would make each heartbeat a successive rotation of these hypothetical "energy spheres."

Time dilates in proportion to scale (I wonder if there's an equation for that...). The smaller something is, the faster time appears to move; the larger something is, the slower time appears to move. We live at the intersection of time, space, energy, etc. And Source energy is the catalyst for all rotations. Below are some videos to help visualize these concepts.

- Watch 3D live MRI or medical animation of the heartbeat. You can almost see the rotation in the muscle firing patterns.

- Now imagine an intersection of two collocated energy spheres rotating in the direction of blood flow. Imagine that rotating energy corresponds with your heartbeat. As your heart pumps, your veins and arteries "light up" as the blood travels with great speed.

- Imagine the spin of subatomic particles (modeled in Earth's spin, solar orbit, the procession of the equinox, and galactic rotation/procession).

Light, Dark, And Void

Within the physical realm, Source energy manifests as pure light. Our consciousness modulates Source light to form matter, just as a projector modulates its light source to form images on a screen. We've been given a similar power of creation as an "intersection of light and dark."

Darkness is not necessarily a substance in-and-of-itself, though everything in the universe is Source. Darkness is merely the absence of light. After all, you don't walk into a well-lit room and "turn on the dark." And consciousness pervades all existence.

When light is absent, the "consciousness of darkness" is no longer held at bay. That's why Shadow exists (in my humble opinion). He is the "consciousness of darkness and shadows." Self-preservation is one of Shadow's most fundamental motivations. Since Shadow is darkness, he needs darkness to spread for his survival. He also needs a "glove box" to use to manipulate the "realms of light." If you find yourself feeling desperate, afraid for your life, or fearful (when you're NOT in actual mortal danger), Shadow is in your "glove box!" The feeling of "self-preservation" is irrelevant to Source.

Let me draw a clear distinction here: darkness and Void are two very different things. Darkness may be the absence of light, but Void is the absence of **everything**. Void is the absence of the concept of absence!

Void is the core of a singularity or a black hole; still, singularities are extremely bright from the light collapsing-in (like the super-massive variety at the center of galaxies). Void is the Source of everything, including light and darkness. Material reality comprises two poles just as "black and white" creates <u>all</u> the shades of "grey" in-between: Even if ½ of matter is Shadow, matter ITSELF only accounts for about 5% of the visible Universe.

There is only light and its absence. But there must be a substrate to reflect the light or absence of it. <u>Einstein</u> conceptualized it as the "fabric of <u>space-time</u>." Modern physics postulate the presence of "dark matter" throughout the Universe. That's why the vacuum of space is NOT considered void. The difference between Void and darkness is that Void is the Source of light and darkness, yet contains neither.

There's no such thing as "want" when you have infinite possibilities.

Fields

Given our ability to "sing" particles in and out of position, one purpose of consciousness may be to form and manipulate various types of EM fields. That makes the mind a "multidimensional EM space <u>modulator</u>" ("Marvin" from Mars would be proud).

We live in a 4D reality. What separates "me" from the "external world"? Answer: EM fields. The "illusion of solid matter" is the interaction between energy fields and suspended particles. We don't fall through the ground or walk through brick walls because consensus reality dictates that the Earth, bricks, and human EM fields tend to remain separate (though we're made of the same stuff, literally and figuratively). The visceral sensations we experience when "touching" "solid matter" are nothing more than the attraction or repulsion of the object's EM fields.

Theoretically, one could modulate their EM fields fast enough to pass through objects, levitate, transfigure, etc. The "stuff" inside the human's EM fields would not be impacted because it's already in a state of constant motion (or quantum superposition). Remember, subatomic particles are 99.999999999% "empty" space (give or take a "9"). There's MORE than enough room for all of "your" particles to maintain cohesion while passing through another object of similar density. Perhaps the high-speed modulation makes particles more "gaseous" or "liquid" to pass through the wall. Your fields and those of others are self-contained and independent of each other, despite having the same energetic substrate.

Physical matter is a collapsed waveform, spinning the possibility that aligns best with our consciousness' expectations. It's a combination of probability and possibility. If reality is made of the same stuff, have you ever wondered: "How do all the atoms that form my body know they belong to "me" and not the ground, the chair, the air, or my clothes?" I'd like to present two hypotheses:

1) Of course, it's physically impossible for two particles in identical states to exist in the same space. But reality is multidimensional. As it is, we maintain cohesion because we imprint our unique "carrier signal" on the subset of particles that constitute our bodies in this

dimension. That means "you" could remain "you" when passing through a wall instead of becoming the wall. If your particles can reach a sufficiently high vibratory rate, you could, theoretically, "phase" through "solid objects," similar to The Flash. The idea is similar to multi-band communication. WARNING: Do not attempt to "phase" unless you have Flash's superpowers.

2) The "stuff" of reality remains fixed while changing states of matter to create the illusion of motion. This is similar to the array of static "pixels" that flash in successive patterns to create the illusion of "motion" on a flat-screen TV. The "energetic substrate" would be a projection, like everything else. In this example, the only things that exist are the illusions of EM fields appearing to move across "stationary" pixels (good luck reassembling your brain after this section).

Time is a curious thing, a chameleon based on its context. From the perspective of the expiration of your "cell suit" when your Light Body returns to Source (AKA physical "death"), time is a curse. In terms of compound interest, time is a gift called "profits." Perhaps that's the genesis of the saying "time is money."

Concepts like "eternity" and "instantaneously" are both meaningless to Source. If you're outside of time, time is irrelevant. Imagine how wealthy you would feel enjoying the company of family and friends, learning, and exploring life with unlimited resources and little-to-no time constraints.

Anything is possible! There is no such thing as "want" when you have infinite possibilities. We need not travel anywhere, physically, unless we choose to do so. All possibilities exist right here, right now with us, in this moment of Now. All realities occupy the same space, simultaneously, on different frequencies (like radio waves, audio EQ, or the light spectrum).

There's a version of the universe where you're living all the possibilities you desire. In fact, we could be "remote viewing" visions of parallel selves living the realities that resonate with our energetic state. When you match the vibration of "that" version of you, you either "phase" into that reality (through harmonic resonance, entrainment, or Huygens' "odd kind of sympathy;"); or, you can think of it as your high vibration creating a "ripple effect" transforming your "external world" into the one in your mind's eye.

We shape fields that hold particles of matter in specific configurations. With a theoretical 1000+fps HoloProjector, movement (locomotion) could require particles to collapse and coalesce in infinite succession. This creates the illusion of <u>motion</u>. But it's an illusion because EVERYTHING is **already** in a state of constant motion. Even the darkness of seemingly "empty" space is in motion. Think of it like this: the space within your atoms is in constant motion WHILE the atoms themselves are moving within the movements of a larger environment called a cell structure, an organ, and an organism. It's movement within movement surrounded by movement.

Motion is constant throughout the universe. As the cliché says, "the only constant is change." Emotion is "energy-in-motion." We move, live, and breathe through "emotion." Since love is the most powerful emotion of all, one could say reality is powered by Divine Love.

PRACTICAL KNOWLEDGE

While you're seeking love outside yourself, everything inside you is begging to be loved.

The InnerMan

We are not the body. We are the spirit/soul that inhabits it. I am the InnerMan living inside this Bioenergetic "space suit" we call a "body." I view consciousness as a property of the InnerMan (or InnerWoman). And as a man, when I speak of consciousness and energy, I'm referring to the InnerMan. When you view life from that perspective, it unlocks clarity that you never thought possible. Envision your "Light Body" just underneath your skin, or "Cell Suit." Your *Light Body* is the REAL "you." Your physical body is merely a "glove box" for your Light Body in this dimension.

Your Light Body has all your human senses and many others that transcend the physical body. The Ancient Egyptians believed that <u>humans</u> (referring to our Light Bodies) have 360 senses, like degrees in a circle. For more information, I strongly recommend watching "The <u>Pyramid Code</u>," (Episode 4, The Empowered Human) to understand better what our ancestors believed about our true potential.

It's All About Now

We all know that living in the "now" or the "present" is a gift. It's not about what you used to be or do; it's about who you are and what you do <u>now</u> that matters most. Regarding your physical body, you are what you eat. It's a literal statement, as your body is built from what you ingest, literally (think about that next time you have a fast-food craving).

You are what you ate. But what many of us forget is that *you are what you hate.*

Since everything external reflects the internal, you hate the corresponding part <u>within you</u> each time you hate something outside you.

By replaying painful memories in your mind's eye, you wallow in the corresponding emotional state, which creates more of the same. In that state, you're "living in the past." Conversely, if you love everything "outside" of you, you love yourself from the outside-in, creating more of the same. While *you're seeking love outside yourself, everything inside you is begging to be loved. That is the definition of true loneliness.* But the answer has been within us all along.

The closest you can get to "Perfect Love" is when you love Source, yourself, and others, in as many "now moments" as possible.

Everything happens "Now." Everyone's true essence exists in the Now. Source dwells in the Now. You learn to live in the "now" by practicing meditation. Meditation yields the mindfulness to be fully present. And once you're comfortable living in the "now," you can return to that mental space anytime.

Regarding your marriage, how are you supposed to love someone who's undefined or nebulous? How can you have a relationship with the concept-of-a-person instead of the real person? We do this constantly! We fall in love ("fall" like a "mistake" as opposed to a conscious choice) with the **concept of a person** instead of who they are at their core. It's best to live in the "Now" when your wife's around so you can get to know the real woman. <u>Being present makes the best of your time together.</u> Your love will deepen because it's based on truth. And you'll be pleased when you discover the phenomenal woman you married!

How to listen to intuition?

Practice, practice, practice! Learn by doing. And remember, intuition **wants** to communicate with you. She will guide and teach you how to hear and feel her direction. Start small and build gradually from there. If you're new to this, I strongly encourage you to try this with people other than your wife until you've had lots of practice.

Intuition wants to be heard.

Intuition will teach you how to distinguish her voice. How do we listen to intuition? When you feel an impression or hunch, apply the litmus test of love and compassion, quickly, with a healthy dose of wisdom. If it passes the test, take action; or if you feel prompted to say something, say it. Why not? The key is to follow it to-the-letter, especially if it doesn't make logical sense (those are usually the most profound). If it's coming from your heart (love & compassion) via intuition or inspiration, do it. Apply your mind to execute it well.

While your brain is screaming "no" (from an overactive amygdala after years of abuse), you'll see that everything worked out for the best. Sometimes a word or action from intuition creates great challenges at the outset. But time will reveal that you did/said the right thing at the right time.

Coherence breathing (HeartMath) allows your mind and heart to sync. Then thoughts and intuition become linked. Next, you connect with your core, as infinite awareness. Breathing and visualization help you get in touch with your heart, where intuition resides.

Intuition is like "Mission Control." While you're on your "spacewalk" performing tasks, mission control maintains the "big picture" view. Mission Control is aware of things, far in the distance, that can impact you or your environment. While you're focused on your work, Mission Control is concerned with the larger environment in which the work is being performed, the condition of all participants, and the overall success of the mission. Intuition is your spiritual "Mission Control." It is extremely helpful when navigating this life, especially if used from the heart.

While learning, prepare yourself to act on each impulse (in the beginning) to learn to distinguish intuition's voice from others. It takes meditation, mindfulness, awareness, introspection, listening, patience, practice, living in the present, and lots of trial-and-error. Be prepared to use The Cleaning Meditation generously as you learn. Each result is a good result in terms of learning. If you follow-through with a prompt to do or say something and the result appears "negative," journal it and shelve it to allow time to uncover the truth.

Sometimes you'll do or say things that "shake up" situations and they appear to worsen. When the root cause is revealed, you can trace the change back to your words or actions guided by intuition. That's the best feeling of confirmation and vindication! It's also a huge source of gratitude and love towards Intuition and Source.

Here's a shift in perspective: the car driving slowly in front of me (when I'm running late) could save my life or someone else's! They could be an "angel in disguise," delaying my haste to prevent an accident down the road. You'll seldom know the full ramifications of your words and actions until they're processed through time. Once you learn how to perceive intuition, you can allow your intuitive "Mission Control" to guide you to the best option in each situation.

Sexology Principles

Consider the difference between working to earn something priceless versus being endowed with it, and working to protect it. For example, imagine that instead of starting from nothing and working your way to wealth, you've inherited immeasurable wealth and it's yours to safeguard. This fundamental principle alludes to a difference between men and women, in terms of one of all species' most valuable abilities: procreation.

Men are born with the capacity to create millions of reproductive cells (sperm) every single day. Natural selection works to our species advantage, in this case; as, only the best and strongest cells reach the egg. In contrast, women are born with a complete set of reproductive cells (eggs) they begin to lose, each month (actually daily), from puberty until menopause. This is a huge fundamental difference in terms of relationships, sex, and our core motivations.

The male sexual drive is infinite; we're ready and able to procreate, any time (um, I mean, for our species' sake, of course). Women have to protect themselves and their precious stash of eggs for the best suitor to advance the species. This is a primal, subconscious, instinctual force that draws her towards what is or appears to be an "alpha male."

During the gestation period, the expectant mother often has heightened self-preservation, on behalf of the baby. After the baby is born, women have countless abilities to ensure the baby's survival. Women feed babies through their bodies, inside and outside the womb. As a man, just try to wrap your head around that concept. Women are endowed to develop, deliver, and nurture our offspring from suckling to self-sufficient.

As wonderful as sex is, it nearly works itself out of existence by the kids it produces (unless you have proper boundaries and prioritize your marriage). Regardless of how much we love our children, they can be taxing on a marriage. Private time for sex becomes a precious commodity once they arrive. Once fertilization happens, women have no procreational need for sex until after the baby is born (though they *may* still want it). But take heart, you just have to change your approach a bit.

Hunger Vs. Thirst

Men's sex drive is tantamount to a thirst, while women's sex drive is often more like hunger. Fact: humans can go much longer without food than without water. Most women don't know that sex is a thirst for men. They don't know it's a biological need, just like their "biological clock" in their 30s. And despite what Shadow has filled your mind with, most of our wives genuinely care about our sexual fulfillment. Seriously, they do.

Sexual arousal is a linear process for men. This follows the arrangement of our biology. There's a thirst that motivates a sexual encounter (a drink) and concludes with a happy ending (thirst quenched). But women's sexual arousal, like nature, is more of a cycle that need not always end in a climax. Conversely, there's a school of thought stating women are uniquely built to enjoy sex, as they actively mate "out of season." Both are true. Using the hunger analogy, sex is like a 7-course gourmet meal with a salad bar and dessert table! I mean, you don't want to rush through all that deliciousness right?

For women, the goal of a sexual encounter is an emotional connection that facilitates a physical one. For men, the goal of a sexual encounter is a physical connection that facilitates an emotional one. Though it's a recipe for a "catch-22" or stalemate in terms of sex, someone has to break the tie (someone as-in whoever you see in the mirror). Understanding these differences can lead to more compassion, connection, and fulfillment. Since women are the "gatekeepers" of the waters that quench our thirst, focus on connecting with your wife emotionally, so the rest can happen naturally.

Men's Vs. Women's Sexuality

Biologically men "give" to receive pleasure; women "receive" to give pleasure. Men give part of themselves as a gift. Women give the gift of themselves by opening the gates to receive their gift. Since women are the "gatekeepers" in this transaction, the man's job is to create anticipation and excitement for her to "open the gates."

Men's reproductive organs are external. Similarly, men process emotions externally (physical altercations, roughhousing, or "taking action"). Women's reproductive organs are internal; and women tend to process emotions internally (rumination or conversation to clarify what they *feel* *inside*). Everything is on a spectrum with men and women expressing multiple traits. However, the dominant tendencies for heterosexuals follow our biology.

On that note, I respect and love all people, regardless of their race, class, color, gender, sexual orientation, nationality, etc. Most of the principles in this book apply to all relationships. Love is universal and equally available to all. That being said, I am an especially heterosexual man or a hard-core "lesbian" in a man's body!

Bear with me for a moment, and forgive the crude but effective analogy. I know this appears simplistic and we all know how this works, but it's used to illustrate larger principles. In terms of reproduction, men give-up part of their body (sperm) to procreate. Women receive the sperm by allowing it *inside* to reach the egg (also the egg has to allow the sperm *inside* for fertilization to happen).

When you're intentional about having children, it increases your chances of fertilization (my hypothesis only) to align your mental images of the child you both want before and throughout your loving union. This aligns your intentions and combines you and your wife's creative powers in the most sacred way. There are no guarantees with fertility, but this can increase your chance of success. If you've already tracked and charted every detail of her cycle and he's been "careful" to keep his sperm-count high, it can help to use energetic principles. There's nothing to lose, but a "bundle of joy" to gain!

Following the gatekeeper analogy, there are three (3) gates involved in purposeful procreation: Gate 1: Her Heart; Gate 2: Her

Body; 3: The Egg. With verbal communication, men give by "paying" attention, giving validation, and offering support. Women receive, which creates an emotional connection that allows them to give themselves to the man. Love is the key to her heart (Gate 1) and often Gate 2. What's cool about gates is that they maintain a secure perimeter while allowing easy access for welcomed guests. And gates are in place to protect something valuable.

Sex, like communication, requires "give and take." During sex, a man feels intense pleasure from the sensations of what surrounds him. "Probing" is a man's default form of communication. It's brief, direct, and goal-oriented. In contrast, a woman feels pleasure from processing the sensations of bringing something inside her body. "Conversation" is her default communication strategy (verbalizing what's inside). It's vibrant, expressive, and interconnected, where the goal of the conversation IS the conversation. It's the difference between expelling vs. absorbing or giving vs. receiving (men vs. women, respectively) as the basis for creating offspring.

Emotions are the key to her "gates." If you can push her emotions one way, then pull them in another, you'll make her obsessed with you. This "push-pull" dynamic is key to building sexual tension (or anticipation) to encourage her to roll out the "welcome wagon" when you arrive at the gates!

Putting Yourself in Her Shoes

Guys, the two most important things you can do for your relationship are 1) put what you're thinking, feeling, and intending into words and verbalize them to your woman, and 2) Look at your words and actions from her perspective. To accomplish this, you'll need a deep understanding of her perspective. The best way is through conversation, questioning, and research.

Let's draw a clear distinction. Seeing things from someone else's perspective differs from "putting yourself in their shoes." The latter is usually destructive. I mean, seriously. If you try to put your size 13's into her size 8 shoes; you'll have to buy her new shoes! The phrase "putting yourself in someone else's shoes" means you're looking at their situation through **your** thoughts, feelings, history, judgments, biases, etc.

Instead, look at your words and actions through **her** life experiences, beliefs, history, feelings, judgments, and more. Or better yet, allow her to tell you, in her words, by asking her non-judgmental questions. That gives you the best chance of having a true understanding from her perspective.

The Power of Our Words

What you verbalize, you visualize; what you visualize, you emotionalize; what you emotionalize, you realize. Verbalization is translating concepts, images, and feelings into words. This can be with our vocal chords and/or our inner voice. ALWAYS REMEMBER: your inner voice has tremendous power, much more power than your physical voice. If you link the two, you've got a "million-dollar mouthpiece."

Our "self-talk" has real, tangible consequences. We allow our self-talk to say things to us that we would **never** tolerate from another person (time for "<u>The Diamond Rule</u>"). I have good and bad news though: the more you connect with Source, the more you can create with your inner voice. It's bad news because you must monitor your thought-life and be intentional with your vision.

Start by saying compassionate and kind things to yourself, instead of beating yourself up. The longer you've been beating yourself up, the longer it will take to make the shift to more positive self-talk. This is powerful, and it comes with immense responsibility. This knowledge can be VERY dangerous for the "uninitiated," or those who do not have control of their "thought life" and self-talk. It's like the difference between handing a loaded automatic pistol to someone who's never seen a firearm (uninitiated) versus a Force Recon Sniper (expert). That's why this information is for those who have completed the EC course or shown enough spiritual maturity to handle the truth. <u>You need knowledge, skill, and experience to use these powerful tools properly.</u> That being said, anyone without a bed (homeless), in a hospital bed or, repentant in a jail cell is "pre-qualified" to use these tools. The spiritual maturity that suffering brings is undeniable.

Studies show that 95% of children up to age three rate as highly creative. By the age of seven, it drops to less than 5%. When researchers dug deeper, they found that, by age seven, the average child has heard 'no' thousands of times. Many gave up their <u>creativity</u> and learned how to conform to receive praise and acceptance. This shows the power of a single word, and it's humbling. Words become beliefs that guide feelings and behavior.

Use your inner and outer voice to speak love into yourself, others, and situations. You cannot attract high-energy results with a low-energy vessel. Be sure your words give life instead of the opposite. Our self-identity must match our destiny!

...focus on the Source of the provision, not the actual provision.

Money is Energy

Since money is one of the most common causes of conflict that leads to divorce, it's worthwhile to address the subject. With all this discussion on energy, it's important to show the connection with this necessary tool of the fiat system: Money is a concept of value with various arbitrary physical objects to represent it. Technically, money is like a "promissory note" regarding value that everyone playing "the money game" agrees to honor. In America, money is a consensus assignment of value delineated using a Base-10 number system.

We've established that physical matter and thoughts are energy. Condensed thoughts are concepts or beliefs. Money is a concept of value. Simply put, <u>Money is energy</u>. Since everything is energy (including you and I) and energy is infinite, one could say we <u>are</u> infinite money (AKA wealthy)! You can stop striving and working so hard for wealth and accept that you embody wealth right now!

The energy that is "money" exists in gargantuan quantities, everywhere. But since it's only a concept, it's infinite. Let's bring this back down to earth. Imagine the amount of money in <u>circulation</u> this very second. I've heard anywhere from $5 trillion to $80 trillion in terms of the global liquid currency in an endlessly flowing "river."

With this expanded perspective, you can decide what your relationship with money will be. Is it a veritable "love-hate," "cops-and-robbers," or "a tool for gratitude and appreciation" type of relationship? Or is it a "tragedy of unrequited love and martyrdom?" YOU determine the type and quality of your financial life.

I like to think of money as a "vote" for the quality of another human's work and to quantify appreciation. But money <u>only</u> applies to humans. The insect, animal, plant, aquatic, and nearly every other natural "kingdom" doesn't recognize our money. Love is the "currency" of life that you can "cash-in" for harmony, peace, joy, kindness, compassion, and more.

Enough Is Enough

What is "enough" money? That's for YOU to decide. And you **must** know the specific amount you consider "enough." "Enough" is an undefined variable based on your lifestyle, interests, goals, etc. You'll never have "enough" if you never define it. Keep it in perspective. **Human beings HAVE and create value, not money**. Money is nothing more than a tool. Can you imagine your crescent wrench ruling your life?

Use spreadsheets, apps, hire a legit professional online, contact a trusted friend or accounting student, hire a financial advisor, and do whatever it takes to get control of money so it doesn't control you. The rule is this: only accept financial advice from someone who's in a better financial position than you.

We know that stockpiles of money can invite unwanted attention. Though a bank account with more than enough is wonderful, it's better to have access to tremendous wealth distributed across multiple investments. Don't be obsessed with "how to make money," but make money work <u>for</u> you instead. Instead, focus on adding real value to others and yourself. In your efforts, be careful not to make <u>money your source</u>, in place of Source.

Good people SHOULD have the most money because they're most likely to use it to bless others. The danger to anyone's spiritual life is becoming overly attached to physical things. The homes, cars, clothes, games, drugs, gambling, indulgences, creature comforts, status symbols, and our physical bodies are ALL left behind when we "return to Source" or "die."

Source Of Money

Everything emanates from Source, and we are all made of the same stuff. Everything is 99.9999999% light. Thus, everything you want is 99.9999999% light. You are a field of energy operating in a larger field, within even larger energy fields. And you are a larger energy field with smaller fields within even smaller fields. We live at the intersection of the infinite and infinite.

Quantum physicists theorize that there's enough energy in the vacuum of a light bulb to boil all the oceans on the planet! If we come from Source, aren't we considered offspring of Source? A cat gives birth to kittens, birds beget birds, and apple trees grow apples. We are neither the totality nor the fullness of Source, but pure logic cannot deny the Divinity within us if we believe in a Divine Source.

The greatest deception from Shadow is to make us forget our Divinity. For example, a cup of the Nile River is sealed in an airtight container and flown anywhere on or off this planet. If we stopped by Mars, it would be asinine for Martians to claim that the container had Martian water simply because it's on their planet now, right?

You came from Source to the Earth, and you're still part of Source, just like the Earth that Source sang into existence.

What does this have to do with money? Source is the origin of EVERYTHING. Source is where we should go for money/resources, instead of trusting in jobs, investments, savings, retirement, people, planning, hard work, etc. Though Source may use these as tools to provide everything we need, focus on the Source of the provision, NOT the actual provision. Don't get it twisted!

Everything comes from Source. On the other hand, the concept of "money" is a human invention. The Genesis Story says God gave humans the entire planet, with an abundance of everything we need. Money is unnecessary in "The Garden of Eden" when you're surrounded by an infinitely renewable food source, natural options for shelter, infinite sources of energy generation (solar, wind, hydroelectric, geothermal, gravity, etc), animals, plants, and everything we've been given on this planet. Also, we are part of and connected to Source. Our bodies are mere containers of Source's energy from the "river of consciousness."

The only major difference between you and everything else in physical reality is:

1. The number and position of common constituents, and
2. Their rate of vibration

Everything we want IS **already within us**; to manifest anything, resonate with it to bring it forth from within. Since we are infinite money, we have immeasurable wealth, right now. Therefore, we can approach Source with gratitude for all the wealth we have now, instead of incessant asking.

What if we approached Source with nothing but gratitude for all we have? Even while envisioning things we "want," we can enjoy the visions in our mind's eye knowing that thoughts-are-things in terms of their impact on reality. We have unshakable confidence because we know our vision, or something unimaginably better, is formed the instant we ask. It is now our job to bring it to fruition, or "birth" the vision through faith and love.

All of our visions manifest "instantaneously" in the energy realm. It's not a fantasy you see in your imagination, it's a vision of a parallel reality in a nearby dimension that exists! There is a version of "you" that has everything that "you" could imagine! With that in mind, you can come from a place of "having" instead of "lacking."

You know Source wants the best for you, just as you want the best for all the cells in your body, your children, and all the cells in their body. Source energy is wealth! Put the energy of wealth to work for you and remove whatever's blocking the floodgates from bursting wide open in your life!

A Perspective on Source

You are NEVER EVER alone. Never ever?? Yes, never ever! Besides Source surrounding and indwelling us, we are symbiotic beings sharing our body with trillions of organisms while surrounded by countless more. We share life energies and can tap into their "ancient wisdom."

Imagine the perspective of a mitochondrion (let's call him "Mitch") living inside just one of your cells (FYI, each cell has numerous). First, Mitch is very ancient... very, very ancient. From Mitch's perspective, everything surrounding him, his "external" environment, is "you" and <u>your</u> cells. To Mitch, your thoughts exist everywhere. Your soul, spirit, body, and presence are **everywhere**.

Mitch knows he's made from the same "stuff" as his surrounding environment (which is your body), just as we're made from the clay of the Earth. In this analogy, "Mitch" knows everything in his environment loves him and has his best interests at heart. You love all your cells, right? Now, apply this analogy to our relationship with <u>Source</u>!

TOOLS & SKILLS

She does <u>not</u> need to be fixed, just loved, accepted, and supported!

Love Provider Precision Tools

As men, we **love** tools; but these aren't just any tools... these are "precision tools" specifically engineered to repair and strengthen your marriage.

- Communication Studies

- How To Validate

- Apply Your Mind

- Engender Love Intentionally

- Just Find Out

- In Case Of Emergency

Communication Studies

Communication is one of the most important skills in successful relationships, especially marriage. Women are natural masters at this. But it's not as easy for us. Ok. So what? Get over it! Now, take responsibility for your side and learn the skills instead of dreaming up more excuses:

Verbal Vs. Written

Simple Verbal Communication:

(1) *Send* > Receive/*Send*
(2) Receive/*Send* <=>
    Receive/*Send*
(3) Receive...

> A good conversation is like a miniskirt; short enough to retain interest, but long enough to cover the subject.

In the above structure, (1) someone initiates a "Send." (2) The receiver interprets the message while sending verbal and non-verbal cues called "feedback." (3) The exchange continues until one or both choose to end communication.

Communication always starts with a sender and ends with a receiver who terminates the session. <u>Do not withdraw and be the one who always ends conversations</u>! Hang-in-there and be present. Be honest.

And verbalize what's in your heart with <u>love</u> and <u>non-judgment</u>. That's the simple definition of positive communication.

Communication Platforms

In-Person	Video Conference	Phone	Text/Email

+ ◄───► -

In-Person and Video Conferencing (like Skype or FaceTime) are superior because they include audio **and visual**. This is vital to ensure that messages are encoded and decoded as intended. In-Person, Video Conference, and Phone Communication have the added benefit of near-immediate feedback from the other person.

For this reason, *use Text/Email sparingly* and <u>VERY CAREFULLY</u>. Phone calls are better than Text/Email but not as good as In-Person and Video Conference. Remember, **it's often better to journal and save the discussion until you can speak in-person.**

There is another "hidden" platform that's a "secret weapon," as it's becoming less common in this technological age (which makes it even <u>more</u> special): *handwritten communication*. Write a note, poem, joke, or inspiring quote on a greeting card or special paper. Give her a handwritten letter, in your ***best handwriting*** (it doesn't work if it's illegible). This is best used sparingly to keep it "special." But it's very meaningful to most women. If you're artistic in any way, you have one of the <u>ultimate platforms</u> to express yourself! In sum, use your gifts, talents, and skills to share your innermost thoughts and feelings (AKA vulnerability).

Nonverbals

<u>The power is in the palm of your hands</u>! Study <u>nonverbal communication</u>! Research it, analyze it. It is the single greatest influence on the quality of communication.

After studying nonverbal communication in college, I found it to be one of the most valuable and applicable subjects I learned. Study voice inflection, facial expressions, volume, tone, body language, posture, hand gestures, eye movements, etc. Realize how your words come across and are likely perceived by the listener.

Micro-expressions are **ABSOLUTE GOLD**! When you learn about these, you'll be able to read people easier than the words on this page!

Listening

Listening is a SKILL! And it's the single most important communication skill of them all! It takes lots of work and time. Listening is NOT only hearing. Listening is not a passive act. And like any skill, it can be improved.

Hearing is a biological sensory experience of decoding sound waves into nerve impulses interpreted by the brain. Conversely, listening is about engaging the brain to comprehend and find shared meaning in what we hear. It takes great mental effort, attention, focus, time, commitment, non-judgment, compassion, patience, and **lots** of practice. The good news: you can practice it anytime, anywhere, and with anyone. It may NOT be an easy skill to develop, but it's worth its weight in diamonds!

Listening is an entire discipline, and I encourage you to study it extensively. For now, you can "fake it 'til you make it" by keeping your mouth shut while giving the speaker your **full attention and appropriate eye contact**.

Listening is an active process where one gives appropriate feedback to the speaker while ensuring comprehension of their intended message. Usually men have much less trouble learning how to listen than learning what to say. As you're developing your listening skills with women, the single most important ability to develop is how to **validate emotions**.

The goal of the female conversation IS the conversation.

How to Validate

(For Men)

Concept: Women live and operate within the invisible realms of emotions. To meet on common ground and fulfill her greatest need for emotional connection and security, you must learn how to validate her emotions through "female-style" conversation. I say "female-style" to distinguish it from what men consider "conversation." If you haven't noticed, they are quite different. Male conversation resembles the "Send <=> Receive" example at the beginning of this section: simple, direct, straightforward, efficient, productive, etc. Female conversation resembles a "maze" of underlined interconnected wires that never detangle, while adding more wires and connections daily. This is similar to how neuroplasticity works in the human brain. In this way, we have a model with which to understand how "female-style" conversation works.

Why learn to validate? Just as men thrive from appreciation and admiration, women's equivalent is emotional validation through meaningful conversation. You can share thoughts or interject ideas when appropriate (or when asked); but be careful not to "commandeer" the conversation. Be sure to relate your replies to your listening, validating, and questions. The conversation is a very meaningful gift to her. And she is likely more adept at it anyway. Let her lead while you listen and learn.

The opposite of validation is "fixing." And even if you offer the most brilliant solution ever conceived, she won't fully accept it because she didn't discover it *on her own*. It's much better to skillfully make solutions HER idea. It boosts her self-confidence while you both enjoy the benefit of the solution, with less conflict. HOWEVER, solutions are seldom the goal of female conversation; rather, it's the emotional connection.

Ideal Goal: She feels understood, accepted, and loved. If she hasn't discovered a solution yet, she's motivated to find it. You want her to gain clarity on her feelings and find solutions that *feel* right to her. YOUR SOLUTIONS ARE NOT REQUIRED for good conversation.

The goal of the female conversation **IS** the conversation. If she leaves a conversation feeling validated without finding solutions, that's a huge win! If you did your job well, she'll find **her own solutions** as she works through her emotions.

The only time you may offer a solution is if she asks you, directly. But if you're skilled enough, you'll answer in a way that allows her to reach her conclusions. Example: She's talking about frustrations with a female coworker, and asks, "What do you think?" You respond, "Wow that sounds frustrating; I wonder if she knows how you feel about this..."

Contrast that with the standard male response, "well, why don't you just tell her how much it bothers you?" (Insert face-palm here). Nice job genius; now she probably feels misunderstood, rejected, and unloved because you **had** to offer your "brilliant" solution. Always remember, **SHE DOES NOT NEED TO BE FIXED!** Repeat, she does <u>not</u> need to be fixed, just loved, accepted, and supported!

Now that you've shifted your perspective on validation, do you see how condescending the standard male response sounds? I guarantee she thought of the obvious solution. She's just hesitant to act because her feelings are clouding the issue, making her doubt herself or get stuck in rumination. Usually the problem solves itself when her emotions are properly confirmed and processed (the "male translation" of validation).

You know you're doing it right when she's smiling, wide-eyed, animated, talking fast, emotive, expressive, and/or enjoying her time with you. When it's your turn to talk, share your thoughts and **feelings** in a 100% honest way with <u>zero judgment</u> of her (use the phrase "I'm feeling___" NOT "I feel like___"). Women can smell judgment like blood in the water to sharks.

Emulate how she spoke with you and discuss your feelings (<u>subtlety</u> is a must). Just be sure there's zero judgment; otherwise, it may come across as you mocking her (bad idea). Always show her 100% acceptance and take 100% responsibility for <u>your</u> feelings and failings. This shows strength and vulnerability, traits that attract most women.

As men, we *facilitate* the conversation rather than lead it. What often sounds like "complaining" to men is her opening up and being <u>vulnerable</u>. Hey knucklehead, **THAT'S A GOOD THING**! If she does this and is met with validation and acceptance (zero judgment), she's more likely to open herself up to you in other ways. (<u>Bow chicka wow wow</u>).

Emotional validation is counterintuitive for men. Men show care and concern by *offering solutions*. We're action-oriented fixers. But remember, there's nothing to "fix" here. Women get stuck and ruminate on emotions. So, validation equals love, care, and concern to her. Validation **is not** trying to fix her emotions either (Insert face-palm again); it's letting her know her emotions are valid and normal. Then she'll resolve the issue <u>herself</u>! Often, women need nothing more than a shoulder to cry on or lean on, a hug, or just "lending an ear."

For men, the equivalent of women's emotional validation is like being stuck trying to figure out the next step in a car repair or build project. Imagine a kind and genuine man comes along saying, "Aw man, same thing happened to me. It looks like you've almost got it though! I found that _____ _____ worked for me, and I know you can handle this!" You thank him, follow his suggestion, it works, and you feel great having conquered another step in your project.

Think of it this way: Responding with fixing is the equivalent of the same man in the example above saying, "Dude, you're still stuck on that?! How do you <u>not</u> know how to do that?! Move over, and let me show you how it's done." You'd likely be highly offended and want to punch him in the face!

All joking aside, fixing instead of validating hurts your relationship with a woman. You can't treat her like "one of the guys." Treat her as the intelligent, strong, independent, and capable <u>woman</u> she is!

...you never know when you're face-to-face with God.

Apply Your Mind!

My grandfather (Papa) taught me many things. One of his most powerful lessons was to "apply your mind." Whenever you face a problem or concern, you can throw tremendous resources at it such as time, effort, worry, fear, discussion, and research. Papa suggested a "free" option that provides the best chance of finding a solution: question yourself and **apply your mind** to find solutions. In other words, use your intellect, life experience, and wisdom to envision viable options.

Next, "test" the options in your mind, with as many variables as you can consider. Use these "thought experiments" for a measured time and journal your results. "Sleep on it" and allow your subconscious to process the questions overnight. The next day, see what your mind/intuition comes up with. With practice, you can do this in the moment (obviously without the overnight part).

When you find solutions within your mind (InnerMan), it's easier to manifest them. This also provides details on which to apply the

Cleaning Meditation. Indeed, the Cleaning Meditation itself is a powerful way to 'apply your mind' to transform your inner and "outer" reality.

Engender Love Intentionally

Learn to care about what others care about most. This can be determined by listening intently, research, reading "between the lines," watching for recurring themes, and extrapolation. If there's a question about what they care about most, ask them "What matters most to you in this situation?" You'll often be surprised and inspired by people's answers.

Find out what matters most to your wife in as many areas as possible, over the years. This is a long-term assignment for many months and years. (BTW, *the best way to "endure" rough times is to have long-term marriage and family goals*). For this to work and not come across as fake or manipulative, your interest in the topic MUST BE GENUINE. Study the topic individually and learn to appreciate it.

Once you have a genuine interest in the topic, drop brief comments about it in casual conversation with her. If it's a topic you don't care about at all, think of it from her perspective. Ask her what she loves most about the topic. She'll appreciate that you cared enough to ask and likely enjoys discussing it. When she sees that you love what she loves, her love for you will grow, as well! (Hint ladies: This goes both ways 3-fold with men).

One universal topic most mothers care about is their kids, for obvious reasons. Keep it positive, light, non-judgmental, and loving. And if they're your kids too, it's a huge win (for you, the wife and kids/family/community) to understand and appreciate them as their dad!

JUST FIND OUT

Often, we do not know how our spouse feels about us, or we think they don't like something about who we are. Often, these assumptions are very wrong. When you reach a point where your communication is high quality and positive, ask her (**_with ZERO judgment_**) directly about the specific issue. Be sure to provide a brief context, so she understands your intentions for asking. The idea is to seek confirmation before you "go off the deep end," mentally or emotionally (AKA "Confirmation Subroutine" in the forthcoming Action Guide). Once I clarified issues, I can't tell you how freeing and healing it was!

Use this technique **sparingly**, and only for the most important issues. I recommend only twice per year (preferably less). If used too often, it can make her feel insecure or view you as insecure. For example, I discovered that many of our marital issues boiled down to my insecurities about my wife's feelings about me. After tremendous journaling and meditation, I broached the subject with her and asked direct questions to confirm if my thoughts were true.

I asked if she still wanted to be married to me and if she was satisfied in our marriage? She worked through some natural reactions to being asked such questions and answered a sincere "yes" to both. That marked a major turning point for us, as I was better able to squash my fears and insecurities.

After you get your answer, it's your job to work towards accepting it. ***Do not use this technique too often and do not repeat the same questions***. This is a once or twice thing. And, before you ask, distill the issues down to the core root to be sure it's a question worth asking. Don't waste this on trivial matters.

Shadow loves to twist things to infuse our minds with all kinds of nonsense. Most of the time, we can address issues in our thoughts and prevent unnecessary tension over something that doesn't exist. Turn on the light, expose Shadow's lies for what they are, and embrace truth in your marriage.

~~*

Life and death is one choice away.

In Case Of Emergency

Love Provider is based on one premise: everything in life has a spiritual basis. How did I come to this conclusion? After struggling with suicidal depression for decades, I tried everything I could find in this world and beyond for help (anything that wasn't immoral or exorbitantly expensive). The techniques that made the greatest positive impacts were always metaphysical or spiritual in-nature.

Spirituality transcends the physical and emotional. Though, biologically, there's great value in understanding the machinery of our "glove box" bodies, it's merely your soul/spirit's immediate environment. And I submit that spirituality is the root cause and solution to nearly every problem in your life.

I'm forever the researcher and student of Life. Perhaps spirituality speaks best to my soul. Plus, the spiritual path reveals the immense value WE EACH have in this world...a message that's perfect for a time such as this. But if something else speaks best to you, WONDERFUL! I support any method that's safe and helps you heal.

After reading countless books on every subject imaginable and trying their suggestions, nothing addressed the "root cause", as the issues kept reappearing like <u>Groundhogs Day</u>. I found real answers in ancient and modern spiritual traditions, prayer, and transcendental meditation. I received answers to my deepest questions that provided much-needed healing in my life.

After finding success in my marriage and mental life (and seeing the same in others), it confirmed my hypothesis again when I took the SITH class. From the Ho'oponopono perspective, the root cause IS spiritual, as is the solution.

As an EC coach, I had a rare opportunity to see if this spiritual approach would help others in similar situations, and it did! From heartfelt discussions with men and women around the US, Caribbean Islands, Japan, UK, Australia, and South America (with individuals from equally diverse backgrounds, ages, and cultures), I noticed uncanny similarities that couldn't be explained through conventional means. However, a spiritual explanation fits like a "glove box!"

Live to love another day!

Throughout the healing and rebuilding process, there were more "emergencies" than I can count (especially throughout the writing, editing, and publishing of this book). One minute things are wonderful, the next my foot is firmly lodged in my mouth (or hers up my ass) and things explode again!

I had to develop strategies to get through these emergencies to "live to fight another day." That was my mantra during my lowest moments. Now, I've "rebranded" the mantra to "live to *love* another day!"

The following are the "In Case Of Emergency" strategies I used to survive various crises to see the next sunrise:

Emergency Types

Marriage Crisis:

The most effective strategy I used was to do something educational. It's hard to learn, grow, and discover new things and remain upset. Plan ahead with screenshots, notes, documents, books (electronic and otherwise), flashcards, apps, etc. that has beneficial information. If that's not an option, the next-best strategy is to do a "mini-meditation."

If practicable, remove yourself briefly or create some space to take an mental/emotional break. Respectfully excuse yourself and get some fresh air. If that's not feasible, take three, slow Heart Breaths (counting backwards from 5) right where you are. If you're able (it can be tough when you're emotional), add the InnerSmile!

Go inward (close your eyes, act like you're in deep thought, saying a prayer, or napping) and do the Cleaning Meditation for the situation. DO NOT ATTEMPT WHILE DRIVING OR OPERATING HEAVY MACHINERY.

CALM AND GROUND yourself, then find Common Ground in the situation. Love her spirit even when the rest of her is driving you mad. Remember, she loves you, has goodwill towards you, and has the best intentions at heart. That's your truth, either way.

At the core, you know you love her heart. Focus on her heart and spirit. Whatever it is, IT'S UNINTENTIONAL. You're still learning and it takes time to reprogram conditioned responses. Look past the flesh, emoting, mental gymnastics, and attacks to see the woman you love. Look through the wall she's put up to see her HEART! Remember, she's merely expressing her FEELINGS. Feelings aren't facts, though they often feel like they are. However, to her, they ARE facts.

Have compassion for her. Many of her idiosyncrasies are due to her personality type, love language, upbringing, etc. Get to know her, DEEPLY. Do Personality Tests together and analyze how you complement each other. Do Flag Pages and read your partner's results to them (and vice-versa). Study the results often! And in the midst of the storm, remind yourself that "**this too shall pass.**"

Imagine two random people: Person A "made" Person B furious, and they separate briefly. Person B returns to give Person A a "piece of his/her mind" and is met with love, repentance, forgiveness, gratitude, kindness, and compassion. How long do you think it would take for the flames of Person B's rage to be extinguished?

You cannot overcome wrong with wrongdoing any more than a flamethrower can extinguish fire; it only creates more of the same. You cannot conquer evil with evil. You don't add fuel to the flames;

you throw water on them. And here, the "water" is love, repentance, forgiveness, gratitude, compassion, etc.

Kid Crisis:

I refuse to give energy to any dark possibilities regarding our precious children, so I'll speak in generalities. Regardless of the severity of a situation, CALM AND GROUND! Take a moment to recognize that this is your <u>time to shine</u>. This is where you get to demonstrate your mastery of love and compassion. This is when you can either strengthen or destroy your relationship with your children.

Envision the situation from their point of view. Recall when you were their age; think of how much you didn't know then. No matter what happened, they need to know that **someone** is in their corner and believes in them. That's your job as a Love Provider.

You know how the world treats people. If not you, then WHO will support them? Sometimes holding someone accountable can be the most loving thing to do. But administer consequences with non-judgment, grace, and mercy. Think of all the times you deserved punishment and were shown grace instead.

Be the peacemaker! Stand up for your kids while holding them accountable for their actions. Be the "bigger man" in the situation and make your acceptance of their spirit and compassion for their pain clear above all else. Maintain genuine love to empower them to conquer whatever they're facing.

By far, the most powerful way to show grace and compassion to your children is to reconnect with YOUR INNER CHILD. AND REMEMBER, YOU ARE A CHILD OF GOD! Reach inward to that Divine Love that shows YOU unending grace, mercy, compassion, forgiveness, etc. and receive the "gift of giving" the same to YOUR children. You get to feel just the faintest slight glimmer of a fleeting glimpse of what it feels like to be like God! Imagine how much you're loved and how you would want God to treat you when you've been caught with your hand in life's "cookie jar!"

Life Crisis (Suicidal):

WARNING IF YOU ARE SUICIDAL, GET HELP IMMEDIATELY. DO NOT WAIT, DO NOT HESITATE. YOUR LIFE HAS IMMEASURABLE WORTH! Suicide is one of the leading causes of death, globally. And I believe with everything in me it's one of the most PREVENTABLE causes! Friend, if you feel you want to end your life amid marriage struggles, your marriage MUST take a backseat temporarily while you **save yourself**. There's no marriage if you're dead.

Also, does your wife deserve to hold your life and death in her hands? No, she's not responsible for your pain. Why? Your emotional pain is predominantly internal, right? Only you can control what happens beneath your skin, even if you can't control anything outside it! Your wife doesn't have the power to determine the fate of your immortal soul. Though I strongly disagree that suicide is a one-way ticket to hell, I know the hell-on-earth that drives one to commit suicide **can** be escaped.

National Suicide Prevention Lifeline
(Please add this to your 'Contacts' now)

1-800-273-8255

After you're fully stable and living life again, you may resume your marriage work. Yet, you may (like me) find that most of the work is cleanup. Often, your marriage/family/work issues subside as you become spiritually, mentally, emotionally, and physically healthier.

Review the AFSP 2018 statistics. When I saw these statistics, my first thought was "our Caucasian brothers and sisters are in crisis." White males have the highest overall suicide rate; and nearly 70% of all reported suicide deaths in 2017! It's an injustice and an unmet need we cannot allow to continue. Remember, when anyone suffers, everyone suffers.

This is an opportunity to begin healing race relations and help our brothers and sisters find solutions to their suffering that allow them to live and love life! I don't know if guilt over our ancestor's deeds is a part of this or not; but I'm willing to forgive, 100%. I didn't say forget, because its memory prevents its reoccurrence. But we can forgive our ancestors, as future generations will forgive us. Whether or not someone accepts me because of my skin color, they're loved and forgiven. And I will no longer perpetuate this pain. The buck stops here.

Suicidal ideation is unquestionably nearest and dearest to my heart. From all the struggles I've faced, and through the experiences of family and friends who have struggled with the same, these are the most personal, heartfelt words I have ever written (and probably ever will).

Whether you've felt suicidal or know someone who has, please read the following thoughts carefully. Each time I meet someone who's in or has been to similar depths of hell (or contemplating suicide), I share the following thoughts straight from my heart:

"Though I can't say I know the depth of your pain or what caused it, I've been in similar places before. And if you feel like no one cares about you, understands, or loves you, I can help remedy that right here, right now.

Friend/Brother/Sister, I love you and care about you more than you can imagine. And I'm showing it right now by sharing my heart. I want you to live, even if you feel like no one else does. There ARE answers to whatever you're facing, and so much love to receive and express.

The world needs the unique beauty you possess. We're family, and I always take care of my own. So I'm here to say: 'There's HOPE! Whatever it is, there ARE solutions, and I'm living proof. Let's get you somewhere safe and chat..."

~~*

Bottom line: I want ALL of my family (ALL Creation) to be happy and healthy. Speaking of family, I am so proud of my nephew Taylor who works at a suicide prevention hotline. After losing one of his close friends to suicide, he decided to give back and help prevent this from happening to others. In addition to my nephew's friend, I've known multiple friends and relatives who've attempted suicide. But tragically, I have a former co-worker and friend who ended his life back in 2016.

It shook the whole office when we found out he passed away. No one, including me, saw this coming. One day, my friend and I are laughing over lunch while working on computer upgrades and service requests; the next thing I know, I'm looking at him in a casket bewailed by his family and a room full of coworkers and friends. After the funeral, I vowed never to do that to my family, by my own hand. I also decided to do whatever I can to help prevent this from happening to others. We all "Return Home" or "die" someday. Let's allow it to happen in its own time.

Suicide is a permanent solution to a temporary problem.

Suicide is a "permanent solution to a temporary problem." **And ALL problems are temporary on this plane of existence**.

If you knew the immeasurable worth you and others possess, would you still want to die? Despite knowing my worth, I developed a "tool bag" full of ways to preserve my life during a "crisis of hope."

When I felt death was the only option, I grabbed my "tool bag" and used every tool I had to survive to see the next sunrise:

1. Temporary Problems: What if your problem's solution arrives **the day after** you end your life? Meditate on that and you go sit yo @$$ down somewhere safe!

2. Suicide Funeral: At my coworker's funeral service, the pain of this loss cut straight to everyone's soul. You could see a depth of sorrow in his relative's eyes I've never seen before, even at other funerals. The cries of grief will forever be etched into my memory. It was as if his loved ones were lamenting, down to their bones. It was beyond heartbreaking. After offering hugs and condolences, I took a few moments to reflect on the toll suicide takes on those left behind.

3. Your Children: Research the aftermath of suicide on children and imagine the potential suffering of your children before you step off that ledge. After reading just a few pages of that guide, it broke my heart to consider the impacts. It's an effective deterrent for me. If you care about your kids AT ALL, you must understand the full extent of this cost. Even if you're upset with them, give them grace, mercy, and forgiveness because they're merely a product of their environment. And you can change that environment! Each time you step back from

that ledge (SAFELY remove ammo and store it all securely), put down the firearm, turn off the car and ventilate the garage, put the pills back in the bottle, etc. you're doing a good and honorable thing for yourself and your family. And the world needs more good and honorable people!

Whenever I contemplated my death, I would immediately envision my children's faces standing over my casket or urn of ashes. It stopped me each time! Once I grasped the incredible toll a parent's suicide has on the kids, I promised myself to endure whatever it took until a solution was revealed. Your kids don't deserve that burden; and they bear the full brunt of your choice, despite being innocent in all of this. Choose life for yourself; if that's not enough, choose life for your children so they have **you** to help them navigate the trials of life that we know all too well.

4. Spite Shadow: After decades of suicidal ideation, it was obvious that Shadow wanted me dead from a very early age. Although I did not understand why, it didn't matter. When I realized all the pain Shadow caused me and those I love, I decided to resist Shadow, if only because he wants me dead! And through all the torment, Shadow strengthened my resolve beyond all expectations.

    At that moment, I knew I could handle whatever Shadow threw at me. From that day forward, I did everything in my power to frustrate Shadow. He wants me dead? Then I will live longer than Methuselah just to spite him. And I will ensure that my soul lives forever in paradise! If I catch wind of Shadow's nefarious ideas, I will actively thwart them. Quid pro quo, my dark friend! <u>I've chosen the light</u>!

One day in 2004 when Shadow was trying to make me kill myself, I responded,

"No, I will live. And because of all you've done to me, I will use all my power to reverse your work in my life and as many others as possible. The more you oppose me, the stronger I'll get. The more pain you inflict, the more healing is sent. The more you make me want to die, the more I want to live! I declare your defeat. Your choice is either to step aside and watch me dismantle your empire, or try to oppose me or those I love, and I'll clean you into oblivion even faster!"

For my EC friends: regarding "against energy," if there is EVER a time to bend the "no against energy" rule, it's to save someone's life. I would rather temporarily be against Shadow and live than allow him to win.

5. <u>Love</u>: Though Shadow used my wife to inflict tremendous pain (mostly unbeknownst to her) and vice-versa 100-fold, I knew it wasn't her heart nor intention. I knew my wife loves me and I love her. After taking the EC Live course, I learned that Shadow inflicted pain on us using our own negative memories! In reality, my wife never hurt me. My thoughts about her hurt me; she merely triggered me to hurt myself and allow Shadow to hurt us. Often, the other

person did nothing to harm us; it was <u>our</u> thoughts that caused harm (meditate on that too).

My wife is the love of my life and I am hers. There was something in the way, preventing our love from reaching each other, as intended. Therefore I decided to find and eliminate the barrier to our love, and that meant thwarting Shadow's plans again. Shadows cannot exist in an environment filled with the light of love. Therefore, remember your true love for each other whenever you face a marriage or life crisis. If you need to hear additional advice about suicidal ideation from a psychiatrist, please view the <u>YouTube video</u> posted by Dr. Peter Breggin.

Life is a trip and no one makes it out alive (at least, not physically). Like everything in this dimension, we all die someday. Why are we so impatient? It's guaranteed to come for us eventually. There's no need to rush the process.

While you lament your life, you're NOT living it! Purpose it within your heart to live life instead of suffering through or merely "existing." Love your life from the driver's seat, NOT the passenger's seats!

Let's ensure that this is NOT your "Final Chapter" but instead "a new beginning." Remember, life and death is one choice away. On one hand, a choice can create life (offspring); conversely, one choice can end life. Will you choose life along with me? Will you choose to love yourself and others? In my humble opinion, there's no better reason to live than to receive and give heartfelt love!

For Empaths

Whenever you feel an internal impression, thought, vision, or vibe, ask yourself: <u>Who or What Am I Feeling?</u>

• A Person	• An Entity	• A Memory
• A Group	• Myself	• God (Source)

Next, try to rule out any biological factor for your visceral feelings or mood. Is it hunger, thirst, sleep deprivation, medicine side effects, hormonal imbalances, loneliness, worry over issues, or an unpleasant memory bubbling up? Once you know where the feeling is coming from, you'll know how best to respond and process the data. Remember, feelings are merely another set of data. They aren't the "end of the world" as they often seem to be.

Love Your Mother!

If we believe in and revere a Creator of everything, including us, should we not love and revere our Mother Earth equally? Motherhood is profound and precious. And the parallels between Mother Earth and our biological Mothers are striking.

Nearly all humans have their mothers to thank for their lives. Without your mother sacrificing months of her life to protect and nurture you, you would not be alive today. She or a surrogate was your sustenance (literally), protector, and teacher for many years, just like Mother Earth.

By protecting their children's "Spark of Life" during gestation, mothers have a connection with their offspring that is second-to-none. I believe our "Spark of Life" lives in our hearts. The pulsation of our heart is evidence. This is just my hypothesis, but I believe the Mother's heartbeat "jump starts" the developing fetuses' first heartbeats. And if you didn't know already, we get all mitochondrial DNA (the "power station" in each of our cells) from our mothers. One could say *our Mothers' love powers every cell in our body!* But it goes much further than that.

Quantum entanglement shows that connections persist regardless of time and distance (it's the basis for the Universe's interconnectedness, as everything came from a single, common point). What kind of connection must moms have with the children they knew <u>before</u> they were born? How connected is the mother's Spark of Life to the Spark of each child she carried and cares for? Even with adoption, mothers give the same love and concern as if she carried and delivered the child herself (Shout-out to my lovely wife and adoptive mothers everywhere)!

Remember, a full-grown human started as only two cells; and our parent's cells formed our bodies, just as we're made from the clay of Mother Earth and our Father's spark of life. Our mothers fed us in the womb which provided the remaining building blocks that formed us. Our mothers WERE our immediate environment during gestation; she was the "universe" that protected us before we entered this realm. At birth, she provides the bacterial covering that protects our skin from the harsh world as we exit the birth canal. She also gifts us many trillions of sentient "micro-helpers" in our digestive tracts that help us extract nutrients from our food.

Your wife is the mother of your children. Honor her as you would honor your mother. And you should love your mother for all the love she showed by virtue of your mere existence...and if you had a poor relationship with your earthly mother, treat your wife with the reverence of Mother Earth. As men and fathers, we need to raise the standard and create a safe and loving world in which our mothers and daughters can thrive!

Inspiration is the only real truth because it comes directly from Source.

The Cleaning Meditation Introduction

Ho'oponopono is a means of reconciliation, as that's what the word means. It's an intensely spiritual method that provides a rich depth of understanding and reconnection with oneself, others, and a higher power. At the core, the basic tenets of Ho'oponopono are based on a love of Source, Self, and Others. This can profoundly change people and situations. Through the transformative power of Divine Love, the Ho'oponopono is an essential tool for LP's. The Cleaning Meditation you're about to learn encapsulates the Ho'oponopono process and many other spiritual and psychological principles.

Cleaning Meditation Acknowledgments

Acknowledgments: The program was created with the utmost love, honor, and respect for Morrnah Nalamaku Simeona, Dr. Ihaleakala Hew Len (Peace of []), the SITH class and instructors, Mr. Larry Bilotta (EC founder), and any other individuals or groups referenced. In addition, I have immense gratitude for Geoffrey at The Center, Billyrose at Vera, T. Russell, T. McTighe, M. Amoo, Tyger L, my brother Ben, Darek Laviolette, Pastor Elder A.J. Watkins, and all my relatives and friends. Most of all, I'm blessed beyond measure to have an incredible wife who inspires me to be my best self and help others do the same.

The SITH class was integral to rebuilding and strengthening my marriage through profound personal healing. It's a modern interpretation of an ancient Hawaiian spiritual tradition that remained untouched for centuries... as if protected on some sort of island or something. ;-)

All your power resides within, not outside. This understanding makes it work. That's why I've focused so heavily on concepts and ideas; it was to prepare you for the Cleaning Meditation. If you're trying to reconcile your marriage, the applicability of this practice is clear.

THE FOLLOWING ARE PERSONAL INTERPRETATIONS, OPINIONS, EXTRAPOLATIONS, AND/OR THEORIES BASED ON WHAT I LEARNED IN EC, THE SITH CLASS, INDEPENDENT RESEARCH, INSPIRATION AND REVELATION. THIS IS AN ORIGINAL INTERPRETATION AND COMMENTARY FOR EDUCATIONAL PURPOSES ONLY.

Ho'oponopono and the Cleaning Meditation

You are about to experience a powerful transcendental meditation that reconnects you to yourself, Divinity, and the Universe. It's obvious why this reconnection is of vital importance in all relationships, especially marriage. Just as envisioning your favorite food triggers your mouth to salivate, or the brain believes you've been heard when you journal envisioned conversations, our imagination is <u>everything</u>!

Most people think of children or artists when they think of imagination. But it's something we use constantly, all day, every day. We use our imagination when giving someone driving directions or recounting a story from our past. We use our imagination while daydreaming at work. Imagination means "mental imagery" NOT necessarily "pretend" or "make-believe."

This is where memories of various ideas and events are replayed by Shadow, relentlessly.

When you envision something, your brain and CNS (Central Nervous system) respond as they would if the event were happening in physical reality. Researchers have measured this in many lab experiments. You can implant, erase, change, and amplify memories in your mind through images, words, and symbols.

Let's revisit some key concepts briefly to provide context for the Ho'oponopono. The following video is an excellent summary of important principles via non-EC and non-Ho'oponopono sources. NOTE: This video references Psych-K, which is another great energy psychology method. These modalities are complimentary.

From a purely scientific standpoint, the Cleaning Meditation is a supercharged, self-induced cognitive hypnotherapy. I've seen some results instantly, and some situations take months or years to clear. However, the transmutation of the emotional charge made it bearable as the long-term issues cleared. It allows you to "hack" your subconscious and disconnect negative emotions from specific memories by taking 100% responsibility and returning the memories to Source, without revisiting (or engaging) the actual memories. Results have been consistent and powerful.

From a religious standpoint, the Cleaning Meditation is a prayer. But it's a "feeling prayer" that reconnects your heart and mind to work in tandem. If I'm cleaning on an interaction with another person, I'll envision apologizing to the person (and/or vice versa) and it's received well. Sometimes we need to "rewrite" memories instead of remove them.

Ho'oponopono roughly means "To Make Right" or "To Reconcile." It's a spiritual practice of "letting go" of memories that cause inner and/or outer conflict by reconciling with yourself, Source, and All Creation. In the Cleaning Meditation, memories are wholly represented by symbols that allow specific memories to be cleaned without engaging them. As the energy changes and thoughts change, the situation transforms, organically.

Dr. Hew Len's idea of 100% responsibility is based on the truth that whatever you experience in life, you're always there. You're the "common denominator" in all your life's issues and situations. By understanding how deeply we're connected, we can effect change for others by working on the part of us that's connected to the shared energy, memory, and/or situation.

IMPORTANT FAQ: taking 100% responsibility does NOT absolve another of all wrongdoing or accountability (though you forgive them and yourself). It's more about focusing on what's 100% within your control: you, your thoughts, and your energy. You cannot control whether someone else feels remorse or repents of their mistakes; but YOU CAN control if **YOU** do. And with all due respect, you were **never** appointed as judge, jury and executioner. Have faith in Source to teach others, as you focus on what Source is teaching you.

In terms of cleaning, who cares who caused it or left it there? The bigger question is "what are you going to do about it?" We can always take responsibility and do our part to resolve it, no matter how big or small the issue. Then, you can heal yourself and others from the inside-out!

For more information on the Ho'oponopono, here's a summary of Joe Vitale's "<u>Zero Limits</u>" book on the subject (highly recommended). One key founder of the modern Ho'oponopono (SITH classes), on whom "Zero Limits" is based, is Dr. Ihaleakala Hew Len.

"A mind that is stretched by a new experience can never go back to its old dimensions."

-Oliver Wendell Holmes, Jr.

The Ancient Hawaiian Ho'oponopono Belief System

There are only two states-of-mind: <u>Memory</u> or <u>Inspiration</u>.

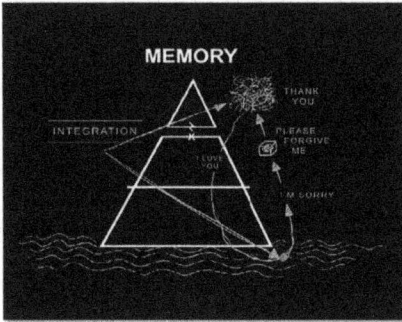

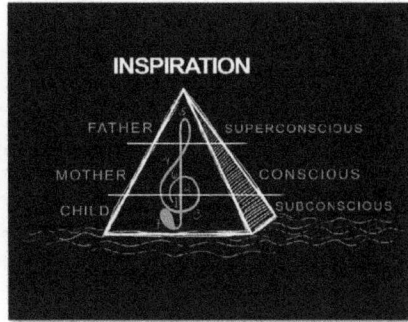

Memory is always outdated. It's where suffering begins, festers, and grows. Memory is where most people spend the majority of their lives, mentally. Conversely, inspiration is joy, freedom, and power. Inspiration means you're connected to Source and receiving advance or real-time guidance in your life from The Designer. Contrarily, Memory provides guidance based on obsolete, incorrect, often misinterpreted, or easily corruptible past information. Shadow and his minions love to manipulate people through tampered and false memories. I am NOT making a case against memories. I'm merely stating that memory is unreliable information on which to base conclusions.

History is one of the most valuable subjects in life. It shares lessons learned by ancestors and inspires new solutions based on past ingenuity. There is great wisdom in studying patterns and historical data. There is great wisdom in learning from mistakes and preventing new ones. All creations, writings, and visions of the past are based on memory. Therefore inspiration is the only real truth because it comes directly from Source.

The Soul Has Three Parts

Super-Conscious	=	Father Energy	=	Aumakua
Conscious	=	Mother Energy	=	Uhane
Subconscious	=	Child Energy	=	Unihipili

Basic Features of Your Soul's Three Parts and Source:

1. **Super-Conscious (Aumakua)** – Your "Higher Self." The highest expression of individuality that's inextricably linked to Source. Aumakua is all-knowing within the realms of Creation and a subset of other dimensions. Masculine "Father" energy.

2. **Conscious (Uhane)** – Your conscious awareness manifest in the "Instant of Now." Short-term and working memory in the moment (like RAM in computers). Nurturing and creative. An active and present waking state. Body consciousness. Feminine "Mother" energy.

3. **Subconscious (Unihipili)** – Your long-term memory. Inextricably linked to Source as the Collective Subconscious. Runs body's autonomic processes. Deep processing and long-term memory. The totality of Creation's illusions.

Masculine or Feminine based on the individual. Impulsive, innocent yet neglected. Child energy.

4. **Source** [] – Original Creator, God, Idolaboth, The All, The Highest-Self. Omnipotent, omniscient, omnipresent, etc. The Source of Truth, Inspiration, and the Spark of Life.

Source is the quintessence of self-sufficiency.

Who is Source?

Despite my Christian background, Source is understood as the beginning of Everything or The Original Void ("before" God's "self-substantiation" from Void). Void is called a "singularity" in modern physics. Recent theories suggest that physical matter enters and exits our dimension through singularities. Some spiritual traditions call it "Idolaboth." Hindus call it Brahma. Gnostics call it "The All." To others, it's the primordial particle of the Big Bang. No matter how you conceptualize Source, it's almost always associated with infinite power, and creativity. The Bible states that "God is Love."(1 John 4:8). Therefore, to Love is to express the attributes of God.

Love is the most powerful healing force in all of existence. As the highest vibration in the physical and many spiritual realms, pure love is the closest we can get to pure Source energy. If you disagree (which is okay), this is not the program for you. And if you are interested in the "dark side," I'll leave you to research that on your own, with _**extreme caution**_.

Note: Light is infinitely more powerful than darkness. To illustrate this, consider a pitch-black room. It's filled with darkness in every square millimeter of unoccupied space. Centrally placed, one light bulb can illuminate the entire room, besides a few object's shadows. In this example, the light was impossibly **outnumbered but not overpowered**.

Here's the "Elephant in the room" regarding Shadow: is darkness part of Source? Though controversial, the answer is in the name: Source. If everything came from and is made of the same stuff, then everything that exists is Source. However, darkness is to Source as the light is to the darkness in the example above. Source IS Consciousness, Thought, Feeling, and infinitely more. Darkness is merely the shadow of all that Source represents. It's the Negative Consciousness, Negative Thought, Negative Feelings, etc. That's how Source is inextricably linked to the super-conscious and subconscious (it also explains why Shadow is so pervasive). Imagine this thought experiment...Source is so powerful, that even It's Shadow is alive! This revelation removes all fear of Shadow and darkness. They're part of the same Source and eliminated with ease through Source's Light.

Consider your favorite dance song on the radio. I guarantee when the bass drops, you can't stay still! Now, imagine cutting all the bass or treble from the speakers. The song won't sound as good. In music, all frequencies contribute to the masterpiece. Just as the light spectrum combines to create holograms, music's frequencies combine to form harmony, consonance, dissonance, dynamics, style, and a mixture of textures throughout the soundscape. As music blasts through your speakers, you're enthralled by the bass, mids, treble, and even inaudible frequencies that create the music. In this analogy, darkness is another frequency in the audio spectrum or color palette. That being said, the highest frequencies are where peace, power, and love dwell. Also, higher-pitched sounds are experienced by the listener as "louder" than an equivalent bass sound.

Here's an esoteric concept you can decide if you believe or not: Besides Love, there is another emotion we can extrapolate about Source from global creation stories: Loneliness. Though Source is the quintessence of self-sufficiency, can you fathom the depth of loneliness of being the only self-aware consciousness in all Creation? Our existence is evidence that love and loneliness motivated Source to remedy it.

Furthermore, the biblical Adam and Eve story tells that God said (Genesis 2:18 paraphrased) "it is not good that the man should be alone…" before creating Eve. God's opinion of loneliness is quite clear. Or God looked upon the man and said, "This guy needs some help!" (Joking ya'll, lighten up!)

This explains why <u>loneliness</u> is such a powerful, deep, core feeling for humans. It can even hasten death! From the <u>elderly</u> to millennials to infants, loneliness is a real issue and a common human experience.

~~*

Consider the bacterium example from earlier ("Mitch"). Everything in its environment is the equivalent of "god" from its perspective; and the bacterium's environment always does what's best for the whole, by default. Your body works to maintain homeostasis at all times. Consciousness either helps or hinders this process. Cleaning restores harmony and equilibrium through reconnecting with Source. Remember, our true "default" state is connection and optimal health.

Consider our offspring: Though human reproductive cells contain the raw materials and "blueprints" necessary to build a full human, *the Spark of Life* comes from Source. Women have the unique capacity to carry two or more sparks of life, simultaneously inside their bodies (AKA pregnancy). Imagine that for a moment... having another separate Spark of Life inside you, next to yours. It takes a special being to handle such a responsibility and privilege. It may be one reason the mother-child bond is so strong. This could also explain why women have a unique spiritual connection and powerful intuition.

What does all this mean? It means Source is everything that surrounds us, while simultaneously indwelling us. Source is our "Spark of Life." This means Source is inside AND outside us. And Source wants everything "in-between" to be at its best, as designed.

Creation is "The Child" that's inextricably linked to Source, just as our kids are linked to us.

Who is The Unihipili?

The Unihipili is what Psychology calls "the inner-child." Though it's the Hawaiian name used within the Ho'oponopono, you can use any name you choose. It's that naïve, yet constantly learning, grandiose yet innocent part of us who loves to play. When its shadow-side is expressed, that's where impulsiveness, impatience, violence, and entitlement come from. You can think of it as a younger "you" embodying humanity's collective subconscious.

Just as "Shadow" is the name and face for the "dark-side," the Unihipili is a name and face for the subconscious mind. Many of us don't know this aspect of ourselves exists! This inner-child was neglected for far too long and needs copious love, compassion, gentleness, kindness, respect, patience, hugs, positive attention, encouragement, affirmations, support, and more.

The Unihipili loves the Cleaning Meditation because it's creative and fun; you're working together to help him/her "clean their room." In this way, parents receive the cleanliness and respect they need while the child's need for positive time and attention is met. Your inner-child loves to create "icons and symbols" to represent energies. The more you delight in the process, the better it works.

It's important to cultivate a positive, healthy, wholesome, pure, and mature relationship with our inner-child to serve the highest good of all. Many of us have tremendous childhood pain that needs to be healed. Since everything in the "external world" is a mirror of the subconscious, one could say "reality" is a direct manifestation of the collective subconscious. If you have unresolved pain and trauma in your subconscious, it will create physical situations that elicit the same pain to feed your "emotional addiction" to it.

Everyone interacts with the collective subconscious as "consensus reality." It's a consensus because we're all equal creators in this dimension. We all agree that the wall is there and the chair is here. But, in reality, both are merely "tactile holograms."

The Unihipili manifests "individuals" as a physical body. That means your physical body, within the "external world," represents your individual subconscious within the collective subconscious; and the Unihipili embodies both. Most of our basic physical desires are a function of our "inner-child."

We're surrounded by crystallized memories, everywhere. In fact, everything we perceive with our senses happened in the immediate to primordial "past." There's a measurable time-delay between a stimulus, the energy traversing space-time, your senses detecting it, and the signal being processed by your brain. Therefore, our physical senses **only** detect the past.

Living beings form complex EM field patterns that endure various timeframes (though nothing physical escapes the effects of decay). An office building is the crystallized memory of its architect's vision.

A book contains the crystallized thoughts of the author. How much more do offspring embody the memory of generations?

Since all of creation is the memory of Source's "fleeting" thought, one could say, Creation is "The Child" that's inextricably linked to Source, just as our kids are linked to us.

Intuition is always nudging us towards Source.

Who is The Uhane?

The Uhane is you, me, and everyone else we know with a personality, sense-of-self, and conscious thought (in most cases). It's the name and face of our present, waking consciousness. It's the mature, high-functioning, logical, reasonable, and vibrant energy of a young adult in their prime.

The Uhane deals with the Instant of Now, the present moment, and what's happening in your environment. This is where "body consciousness" is expressed, not self-consciousness. Body consciousness is the awareness of your body's internal and external sensations and machinations. It's the sense-of-self. The feeling of hunger, thirst, a headache, a paper cut, wind on your face, indigestion, or the inner warmth of a smile are examples of body consciousness. Without it, we wouldn't know when something is right or wrong in our body. It's internal. It's feminine energy, which is why feminine Intuition speaks so effectively to the Uhane (present moment).

Intuition and the Uhane are both feminine energies that love and nurture by default. This may explain why women are often more body-conscious than men. Since women carry and deliver children, their bodies are "the environment" for the developing baby. She must be conscious of what's happening in/around her body to keep her baby safe. The Oracle (Intuition) lives inside The Matrix, just as Intuition lives within the Uhane. And like the Oracle with Neo, intuition is always nudging us towards Source.

I believe that "Intuition" is another name for The Holy Spirit. The Holy Spirit is God's Spirit, just as we each have a spirit. She permeates reality, as our spirit pervades "Mitch the Mitochondrion's" reality.

It's what most people consider their "higher-self"

Who is The Aumakua?

Aumakua is the "inner coach" and advanced executive functions of the mind and soul (Shout out to Tanya @ KAP Therapy). And I'm talking about the best of all the greatest championship coaches of all time, in "God-mode" (Up, Up, Down, Down, Left, Right, Left, Right, B, A, Start-style)!

It's masculine energy, ancient and wise, paternal and overflowing with compassion. Aumakua is the name and face given to the super-consciousness. It's a paternal, "Father" energy. He's our "meta-consciousness" if you will. When I say "Father," I'm talking about a good, good father who embodies all the best of everything a father represents. To all my brothers and sisters with "daddy issues," the answer is as close as your super-conscious. You can reconcile all issues that relate to our earthly mother and father through the corresponding aspects of us. The Aumakua is Father, The Uhane is Mother. Through The Cleaning Meditation, you reconnect both with The Unihipili and Source.

I see the Aumakua as the "Overseer" like Mission Control, or the "Architect's Assistant." This implies there may be a being higher than "The Architect", as in The Matrix (Deus Ex Machina). The Aumakua is not Source, yet far above us in the "Heavenly Hierarchy." He's the "all-seeing," "30k-foot view," protective, wise, and infinitely patient version of you. It's what most people consider their "higher-self."

The Aumakua has a top-level view of Reality surpassed only by Source. Aumakua sees all your past/present/future lives, paths, choices, possibilities, and more. From a higher dimension, this gently authoritative and confident energy provides balance, service, and leadership to the Mother (Uhane) and Child (Unihipili). The Aumakua is an inspiring teacher and a metaphysical "glove box" through which Source can interact directly with us, internally. It's my hypothesis that remote viewing, precognition, telepathy, transcendent wisdom, enlightenment, etc. are all features of the Aumakua.

~~*

What are the implications if all beings are born with this 3-part "template" for the development of "self-identity?" Perhaps, everyone would have "placeholders" for the Unihipili, Uhane, and Aumakua that develop over time.

Following this line-of-thought, there could be life circumstances and traumas that cause one or more of the Unihipili, Uhane, and Aumakua to develop prematurely or slow their development. That would mean one could go their entire natural life without integrating all three parts, connecting with their Higher Self, or developing a personal connection with Source.

That's where the beauty of the Cleaning Meditation resides. It reconnects all aspects of "you" with Source. I say, *"Reconnect" because interconnection is our natural, intended state.* Alignment with Source is our True Default. The healing that comes from this truth, alone, is enough motivation to clean constantly!

In the Cleaning Meditation, the Unihipili, Uhane, and Aumakua work with Source to transmute darkness into light. And when you're connected to your Higher Self, you are unstoppable! Imagine the collective subconscious (i.e. the entire Matrix), the Oracle, The Architect, and The Creator guiding you, moment by moment. This is the truth and power of living in Inspiration!

Light Body

Below is a concept included to illustrate Ho'oponopono ideas that are **unrelated** to the SITH class. However, it is inspired by Ancient Egyptian, Hindu, Buddhist, and many other spiritual traditions.

The "Light Body" is what some call the "astral body." Buddhists discuss the idea of a "rainbow body." It has several layers conceptualized by its name: a body made of pure light. It's the form humans take without physicality. The Light Body encompasses all light spectrums as a "master copy" of your physical body (this means your physical body is a replica of the Light Body). It contains energy vortices called "chakras" where the river of consciousness forms currents and eddies around your "spark of life."

One major difference between the light and physical bodies is that the Light Body remains whole and perfect in every way. If you have *any physical or mental ailments*, realize the truth that they do not exist in your Light Body. It's your "original energetic blueprint" just under your skin, but not bound to it. Like the "twin ghosts" in the Matrix, you (theoretically) could instantly heal yourself by causing your cells to revert to your Light Body "default." If this is true, it could happen through envisioning your Light Body form through a meditation that reconnects you with Source (perhaps).

We can travel through infinite dimensions and realms by "decoupling" our Light Body from the physical during sleep, OBE's, or at death. Some call this "astral projection." The best visual for this is in the Dr. Strange movie. When character's get "knocked out of their body," the result is a great representation of The Light Body. Some say that during our physical lifetime, we're tethered to our physical bodies, so as not to "float away." When our "cell suit" dies, the "tether" is severed. This frees our Light Body to return to the place from which it came, Source. I like to imagine that the Light Body corresponds with the Aumakua (Super-conscious).

In this metaphor, all emotions, visions, sensations, intuition, and thoughts reside within the Light Body. Perhaps all our senses are, in fact, detecting what's happening in our Light Body in response to the environment. If this were true, our CNS (Central Nervous System) detects internal responses to external stimuli...

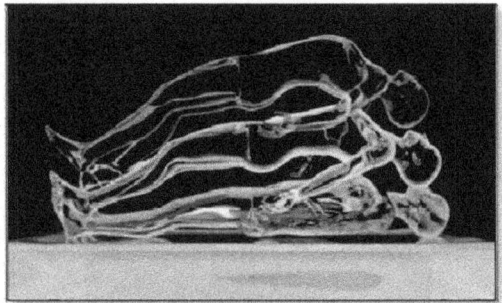

We're each reflections of Source Consciousness (Infinite Awareness). Your soul/spirit is your Consciousness' immediate environment. Your Light Body is your soul/spirit's immediate environment. The physical body is your Light Body's immediate environment.

They are each layers of "you."

Our optimal (AKA "flow") state occurs when we realign all our layers with Source's Love.

Everything your senses detect and your brain interprets as "outside" of you, IS you! It's all part of you, sharing the common substrate of Divine Light. Our Light Bodies walk upon a common substrate of light energy interlaced by a web of energies that exist everywhere! This intrinsic connection facilitates cleaning on anything and everything. The Uhane, Aumakua, and Unihipili have individual intelligence with **unlimited holographic memory storage (morphic resonance fields)**.

We clean by *humbly and lovingly* asking Source to transmute energies associated with the memories found within the Unihipili. In simpler terms, we're requesting an emotional/energetic "Factory Reset" of our subconscious memories throughout all time and space. This occurs via the power of Source's pure light impacting The Matrix of Light that we call "reality."

Your departure from Love disconnects you from your Higher Self

Cleaning Principles and Purpose

When an undesirable childhood, marriage, or other memory "bubbles up" from the Subconscious and replays in your conscious mind. This lowers your energetic state. Source cannot connect with low energies directly (without destroying them). The intermediary that allows connection is love.

When a negative memory is playing, it recreates the associated visceral sensations and negative emotions that "knock you out" of love. *Your departure from Love disconnects you from your Higher Self.*

Since memory is a dramatically lower vibration than Inspiration, you lose your higher connection through entrainment (resonance) with the lower vibration. We call this "engaging a memory," which causes all manner of suffering.

Conversely, when you live in Inspiration, your entire being realigns as an integrated whole. Then you'll do and say things that are perfectly delivered at the right place and time.

Cleaning is an honor and privilege. If it becomes a "burden" or "chore," take a sabbatical, as this is a sign that your heart is weary and/or <u>not</u> in the right place. There's zero judgment in taking a break to heal because your heart is fatigued and/or injured. **Even elite soldiers accept help from medics!**

Cleaning is a service to all Creation because it clears the <u>collective subconscious</u> of negative energies associated with memories. How is this possible? <u>Source does the actual cleaning</u>. When Source cleans something, it's **permanently** clean, beyond the quantum level.

Why would Source do this? An omnipotent, omniscient, omnipresent being of Infinite Love and Creativity knows that problems occur when people have free will. In other words, sh*t happens! To respect our free will, Source desires <u>us</u> to take 100% responsibility and clean whatever is in our path (or "Tend The Garden"). In the Biblical Book of Genesis, Adam and Eve were given

100% responsibility (or dominion) over all Creation. Despite the "forbidden fruit" incident, that responsibility was never revoked.

Here's a visual on which to meditate: **The best way to heal "The Land" is to shoe the feet of all who walk upon it with the Light of Love.**

Why do I talk about love, peace, and compassion so darn much? To answer that, I'd like to provide some background: when the gravity of deliberate creation hit me, the massive power and responsibility <u>landed on me, as well</u>. After extensive trial and error (ok, maybe mostly error), I had to achieve more consistent results. I realized that monitoring every thought and emotion while maintaining deliberate positive visions was exhausting. It's too much data to manage while dealing with everyday life.

I learned that focusing on the highest vibrations makes everything easier, more powerful and effective, more fun, more positive, and more <u>consistent</u>, all at once! Love and compassion change your "default" to create that which aligns with <u>everyone's</u> highest good. As you embody genuine love, peace, compassion, and gratitude, you're given license to shape reality without fear of causing harm, knowing that you'll serve the Highest Good.

Cleaning Fundamentals

It takes approx. 72 hours for new neural pathways to form in our brains. <u>Current research</u> shows it takes over 90 days of consistent effort to form a new <u>habit</u>. Like all good things in life, success is achieved through consistency.

<u>Love the process</u>! The process <u>is</u> the destination. The journey <u>is</u> the goal. Remember, love, compassion, appreciation, gratitude, and enJOYment ARE our true natural state!

Warning: You're uncovering tremendous power and **equally tremendous responsibility**. This power has always been within you, just dormant. From now on, you'll have an unfair advantage in every situation. Therefore, you MUST have humility and compassion, knowing that very few know anything about this until now.

Humility protects you and others from **<u>your</u>** newfound power! The Universe is the Ultimate Professor, and humility prevents your lessons from being too harsh.

DO NOT TAKE THIS RESPONSIBILITY LIGHTLY. I will repeat: **<u>DO NOT TAKE THIS RESPONSIBILITY LIGHTLY</u>**! If you have any hesitations, please stop now or skip this entire section and return to it later. The information is here whenever you're ready.

Below is a brief introduction to the first few techniques used throughout the Cleaning Meditation. You can (and should) practice these constantly:

1. InnerSmile

2. Heart Breath

These two powerful healing practices combine to form one potent process (like Voltron): While taking slow, deep breaths (breathing through either the nose or mouth), envision a huge, cheesy smile filling your chest. Envision your breath entering and leaving your Heart and Solar Plexus through the InnerSmile. Do this as often as possible, every day. This can be done while doing other activities, as long as you and others are safe.

We can either trigger disease or the self-repair process, as the type and quality of our emotions regulate cellular states. This is a healing and life-enhancing practice. Remember, your inner-voice and mental images determine your emotional state. See the HeartMath website for more details and research on Heart-Brain Coherence (Heart Breath).

Practical Meditation

The 7 P's: **P**roper **P**ersonal **P**reparation **P**revents **P**iss **P**oor Performance

1. Quiet & Safe Location (earplugs or headphones, if practical)

2. Timer w/Gentle Alarm* (phone app, watch, or analog) *tested and confirmed functional

I recommend an alarm that's not too startling or loud (yet able to wake you, if you fall asleep). Vibrate mode works well. Be Smart: setup contingency plans for unintentional naps.

Set timer for 3:33 up to 90 minutes. <u>Always check settings</u> **(and that it's on)** <u>before you begin meditation</u>. This allows you to relax and surrender to the process, trusting that your *accurate timer will honor your available time*. Even if you have the luxury of "no time constraints," it's wise to set an alarm to track your meditation times.

•-• Brief Version •-•

Usage: Anytime, Anywhere Safe

Duration: 3:33min (use timer)

1. Touch your heart or Solar Plexus area gently and focus your awareness there.
2. Breathe deeply and slowly through the InnerSmile in your heart (Heart Breath).
3. Cultivate genuine feelings of appreciation, gratitude, love, compassion, wealth, freedom, purpose, etc. within your heart.

•-• Longer Version •-•

Usage: 1-3x Daily Anywhere Safe

Duration:15–90min(use timer)

1. Calm & Ground (Common Ground).
2. Heart Breath & InnerSmile.
3. Stillness & Become Void.
4. Perform the Cleaning Meditation, prayer, or other energy work

Practice <u>each section</u> separately until you're comfortable, THEN add the next

WARNING: The following techniques are intended ONLY to serve the Highest Good of ALL. If you attempt to use for ulterior motives, selfish gain, or nefarious purposes, it **will** backfire on you. This method is based on the "mirror principle" of reality, but it's more like a "magnifying mirror." In other words, it amplifies what you infuse and reflects it back to you. For that reason, this method was designed for use with love, gratitude, repentance, forgiveness, and other "positive" emotions only. Do not alter, add, or subtract anything from the process. Source will direct your use of the meditation.

This transcendental meditation should never be used while driving, operating heavy machinery, or performing any activity requiring your full attention. It's a powerful form of self-induced hypnotherapy. The purpose is to realign self with Source to embody Inspiration. Since we have a common Source, I trust you'll receive guidance on how to apply this in your life from the True Author. This is a "Cult-Free Zone" because everything in this book pertains to your **personal inner spirituality and self-discovery**.

THE CLEANING MEDITATION

The Process

Summary: We begin with deep breathing and proceed through a guided visualization for relaxation, healing, cleansing, empowerment, exploration, reconciliation, inspiration and more. When complete, we return to an expanded waking consciousness.

-SECTION 1-

Deep Relaxation

Begin by focusing on your breath, as the breath of life enters and exits your nostrils, trachea, lungs, and bloodstream. Take 3 - 4 deep breaths, filling every crevasse of your insides with the "Breath of Life." Envision filling with air, from your hair follicles to toes. Inhale light; exhale all darkness (tension, worry, fear, anger, pain). Take your time here, as being open and present is vital to your personal healing. You're safe, on common ground, within a Universe that loves you. Now, <u>Calm and Ground</u> yourself:

- **Calm** – Savor inner peace. You're safe. We're always on common ground connected to everything and everyone.

- **Ground** – 1) Envision standing or seated in river/lake water 2) Picture "roots" growing from your feet into the soil, or 3) Imagine a white light rope connected to the Earth's core, your heart, <u>and</u> the Sun's core (extremely powerful and advanced).

Remember, you're in a safe place. We're merely using our imagination to envision things. Feel free to use 1st Person and 3rd Person points-of-view in your mind's eye. Let go of "fight-or-flight" reflexes. No lion or rhinoceros is chasing you. It's okay to release tension in all your muscles, slow your breathing, and deepen your breath. Sit comfortably, yet unable to fall asleep. If you cannot meditate without falling asleep, your body is telling you it needs time to regenerate (AKA sleep).

Release all tension in your muscles starting with your forehead, eyes, face, and neck. Envision your eyes resting on imaginary plush silk or cloud pillows. Your eyes get heavier, sinking into the pillows as you remain still and relaxed.

Choose a fixed point (either physical or mental) on which to focus your gaze. This keeps your eyes from "wandering" too much. Let your jaw hang freely on its hinges as peace washes over you, head-to-toe. You're relaxed, calm, and safe.

Notice your body's internal sensations while remaining still and relaxed. Imagine that the sensations beneath your skin are your Light Body!

Relax all muscles in your face. Picture a large, diamond-light "halo" descending from above your head down to your toes. Release all tension along the way, as the bright blue-white halo descends to the ground. Enjoy the tranquility flowing from the top of your head down your shoulders, through your lungs and heart, past the intestines, pelvis, and knees, down to the soles of your feet.

Now, envision a golden halo ascending from the ground-up, remaining above your head, forming a golden cylinder of light around you. On the way up, the golden light brings even deeper relaxation down to your bone marrow! You're now seated or standing within a cylinder of golden light that **only** you and Source can enter. You're safe and protected as you continue the visualizations.

Breathe in love; breathe out all negativity so only love remains. Acknowledge any thoughts that come. Allow them to fade away or place them on an imaginary "shelf" for later. When imagining, use vivid and immersive visions, with as many senses as possible (sights, sounds, smells, textures, temperatures, visceral sensations, tastes in detail). Be present in the moment. Allow your mind to be blank, like Void...an empty canvas for you and Source to create a masterpiece. Enter stillness and embody Void.

When visualizing, remember you can bend the "laws" of physics and do anything you can conceive. You can lift any weight, pass-through and see-through any object, teleport, manifest anything, shrink or expand to any size, and experience anything in your mind's eye. You have 100% creative freedom in this process. That's what makes it so much fun!

When you lead with love and compassion, you can make your own rules without causing negative effects during or after the meditation (again, assuming you remain focused on love and compassion).

If you ever get stuck in negativity, **stop immediately**, take a few breaths to refocus, reset, and pick-up where you left-off or start over. Remember, Shadow is always trying to commandeer your thoughts for his purposes. Instead, go inward to your innermost core where Divine Love dwells. Envision diving into the micro-singularities in your protons. Live within Void, from which everything came!

-SECTION 2-

InnerSmile

The InnerSmile is a spiritual practice gleaned from a <u>qigong master</u> named Mantak Chia. It's exactly how it sounds: <u>Smile with your insides</u>. While keeping your face still and relaxed, envision the biggest, cheesiest smile filling your heart/Solar Plexus. Radiate the warmth of the smile throughout your body; send light from your heart-outward in 4D, spherical directions.

Imagine the smile filling your chest. Keep your face still and relaxed and <u>smile with your eyes</u>. It's okay to smile with the rest of your face too. Most women love when you smile at them with your eyes. Feel the warmth and uplifting energy fill you to overflowing. Your body will release the same endorphins as when you're physically <u>smiling</u>.

Maintain your InnerSmile throughout the day alternating with Heart Breath's AND BREAKS (very important, recommend 30-60min). You may combine the InnerSmile with preceding and subsequent steps whenever comfortable.

-SECTION 3-

Heart Breath

To breathe for <u>heart-brain coherence</u>, envision your breath entering and leaving through your heart/Solar Plexus. This can be accomplished by combining the InnerSmile with deep breathing.

Using an <u>odd number pattern (5, 4, 3, 2, 1)</u>, **count backward** slowly while breathing thusly:

1. **Inhale** for 5 counts
2. **Hold** for 5 counts (Optional)
3. **Exhale** for 5 counts
4. **Hold** for 5 counts (Optional)

5-counts are an average starting-point. Feel free to reduce or increase the count to whatever is comfortable for you. The odd number and counting backward engages the brain, forcing you to be present. While remaining present, focus on the Heart Breath, InnerSmile and stillness, save for the

rise and fall of your chest. In the Ho'oponopono, it's called the "Breathing Ha." But I see it as the "Breath of God."

Breathing slowly is a "bio-hack" that signals your cells to enter "self-repair" mode, as you naturally breathe slower when safe or asleep. When you trigger "fight-or-flight" or the "stress response," breathing becomes shallow and you conserve resources for defense and escape (higher blood pressure, diverting blood from non-essential brain and body functions, pausing digestion and reproductive processes, etc.).

Reader, please be safe! If you have ANY physical, mental, emotional, or spiritual problems with any of this, stop and only use whatever is comfortable for you. That being said, don't be surprised if you're challenged, stretched, refined, strengthened, tested, encouraged, and so much more throughout the process.

If you feel slightly light-headed during the breathing exercise, it's okay. Simply pause if it gets too intense; breathe normally until it passes, then start again. As always, consult your trusted physician if you have ANY concerns about using this or any other breathing or meditation technique. If you experience any physical discomfort, vertigo, or shortness-of-breath, discontinue use and seek prompt medical attention. One wise precaution is to use a wearable biometric device to track vitals. ALWAYS have a working phone within reach if you ever need help. With this device, you can see the physiological impacts of your meditation practice, real-time and over-time. Review results after meditation to prevent unnecessary distraction.

-SECTION 4-

Void – Singularity

Become Void in stillness. Tap into the infinite energy from which we're made. Focus your awareness on Source and allow your thoughts to fade into the background. Relish the freedom of being empty, like Void. Like a blank canvas, you're ready for Source to "paint" a masterpiece.

With emptiness, there's nothing to prevent Source from filling you completely!

In Void, there's no pain or bondage; there's nothing, which is the purest form of everything! Allow yourself to lose track of time; you're safe with your timer. You're now prepared to enter pure inspiration, which is the goal of the Ho'oponopono.

Once you're ready, proceed with the <u>Cleaning Meditation</u> or any other spiritual work you'd like to do. Pray and contemplate questions you've asked of intuition; be inspired, visualize, and experience the corresponding emotions and sensations in your body.

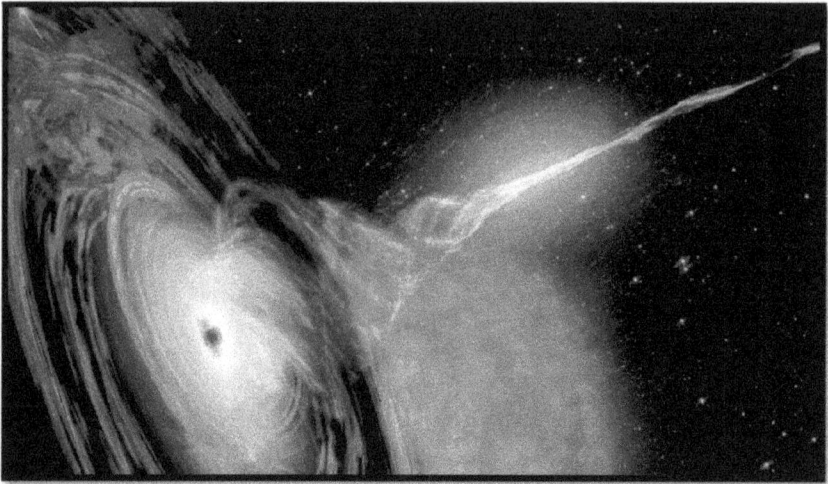

-SECTION 5-

Reintegrate & Finalize

Post-Meditation: <u>This step is crucial</u>. Do not neglect this. Slowly and gradually, transition back into waking consciousness by counting backward from 10 (10, 9, 8, 7, 6, 5, 4, 3, 2, and 1).

Bring your awareness back to the present moment and open your eyes (if closed) when you reach 1. Sit for a while and note any sensations within your body. Take 2-3 deep breaths. When ready, stand-up slowly as you bring your awareness back to the "Now" moment.

Always try to do this step to conclude your meditation. It helps cement your inner work and allows for a positive reentry to waking consciousness. Last, reflect, journal, act upon inspiration, and/or return to your day's activities. If something especially powerful or profound happens, journal, audio record, or video record yourself to remember the experience.

Voice recording is recommended during meditation, if it's not a distraction. Most Smartphones have voice recording apps, or you can install one (name recordings with the subject matter). It's best to save writing until after the meditation; but with practice, you can journal during meditation.

The Cleaning Meditation takes tremendous focus and concentration, especially while learning the process. Once you've practiced the meditation sufficiently, it will become as easy and natural as thinking about your favorite subject. Lastly, allow Inspiration to direct your remaining steps.

The Cleaning Meditation Rationale

Though "you are what you eat," I believe also "you are what you think." The following meditation/visualization is a metaphor for life and the invisible, spiritual realm: Imagine consciousness as an infinite river. All kinds of things float downstream into your awareness. Daily, you cross the stream from "Infinite Island" to your local "town" and back. This represents the transition from unconsciousness to being awake (physically and/or spiritually).

The water in the vision is deep blue and always perfect temperature, calm, knee-height with the deepest part up to your waist. As you walk through the river, you stumble upon various items deposited on the riverbed by you and your neighbors. These "deposits" can be as recent as "Now" to the beginning of time. You're safe here and nothing can harm you in this realm.

These represent memories that "bubble-up" to our awareness (Uhane) from the subconscious (Unihipili). These are the issues that are most important to us and our relationships. This is the case because the Uhane "sings" reality into form based on the type and quality of your emotions. When you're replaying a negative memory, you reenact that emotional state. This, in turn, taints your view of reality or recreates similar dynamics as the negative memory. This is what we call "emotional baggage." However, when you clean, you retain the benefits of lessons-learned without the negative emotions.

You can trust that your Higher Self fully understands your intentions and the purpose of the cleaning, as your Higher Self is a part of you. When you choose a topic, event, or memory you want to clean (the riverbed deposit), give it a short, simple name (like an icon on a computer or a file folder). Use that name when pulling it out of your subconscious. This makes cleaning purposeful, specific, and clarifies intention **without engaging the memory**.

The "icon" represents the totality of the issue, energy, and everything involved. Just as we program computers, we can program our minds with complex instructions that are represented by a word, phrase, or symbol.

Example: Let's say there's a recurring issue with your wife being critical of your actions. Instead of naming it "critical," choose something that's related but more innocuous. Perhaps she frowns while nitpicking; you could name it "The Scowl" or perhaps "The Inspector." The mere act of naming an issue greatly reduces its impacts. Then, you reach into the river and pull-up an object (determined by your subconscious) that represents the energies related to "The Scowl." The object representing "The Scowl" that was lifted out of the water as a "riverbed deposit" can be anything your imagination wants it to be. By removing the energy, you remove the root of the situation. That's how we clean with specificity, but without engaging the actual memories.

Once you learn the underlying principles for each step, you can set an intention to "program" them into your subconscious. This is similar to mental symbols or "icons." You "run the program" by envisioning, saying, or thinking about the "icon." With the Cleaning Meditation, you run a full "cleaning and optimization" utility every time you imagine the steps as a vivid, immersive holographic experience.

Each day reveals new problems and possibilities.

What does all this have to do with marriage?

In relationships, there are numerous past, future, and present challenges. Joys and pains cut straight to our core. In actuality, marriage is the union of two people's entire childhood experiences. We carry all the messages, traumas, lessons, pains, and joys, from our formative years to the present into our marriage. For most, we learned everything we know about marriage from our caregivers, books, and TV/Movies. This forms a "marriage program" that we run with our spouse.

Our "marriage programs" only run under real marriage circumstances. Cohabitating or being engaged seldom initiates the full program. Invariably, the interactions between partners cause tremendous conflict as they enmesh their independent lives into one. With jobs, money, homes, relocation, children, in-laws, health, sex, social lives, temptation, and religion, you have a recipe for steady "deposits" on your subconsciousness' riverbed. The Cleaning Meditation provides a beneficial way to address issues silently in-preparation, on-the-spot, or after a "deposit" is discovered.

The Ho'oponopono inspired the Cleaning Meditation. It's designed to reconcile all types of relationships. In addition to your wife, you reconcile with Source and all other relationships, including yourself. You can reconcile with people, places, and things of the past, present, and future. Whenever problems arise, you have a means to bring about healing and reconciliation.

As we "row, row, row" our boats down the river of life, we have a powerful tool to address any obstacle we face. It's spiritually, emotionally, and psychologically beneficial which positively impacts physiology and biology. With mastery, you can run this "program" instead of your usual anger, hurt, frustration, or other destructive knee-jerk reactions.

Each day reveals new problems <u>and</u> possibilities. The Cleaning Meditation opens a window for true repentance, forgiveness, gratitude, and love to enter any situation and bless everything/everyone involved. Watch as situations that would have previously caused harm become beneficial. Challenges become catalysts bringing people closer to Source and each other. In sum, it "upgrades" your life and relationships.

It's a salubrious spiritual practice that heals the spirit and mind with Love Divine. With this Love, you're equipped to be a Love Provider!

Cleaning Meditation Summary

Preparation: "Name" the memory. Set Timer, InnerSmile/Heart Breath, Stillness. Envision:

1. **Repentance:** *"I'm Sorry"* – Lift memory "icon" out of the Subconscious River.

2. **Forgiveness:** *"Please Forgive Me"* – Let go of the memory asking your Higher Self to package and deliver it to Source to be cleaned.

3. **Gratitude:** *"Thank You"* – Source receives the package from your Higher Self. Gratitude is plentiful between you, Source, and all creation!

4. **Love:** *"I love you"* – Source restores the memory to a pristine state, as Divine light shines into the Subconscious to fill the "hole" from which the memory came.

Thank Source and live in Inspiration!

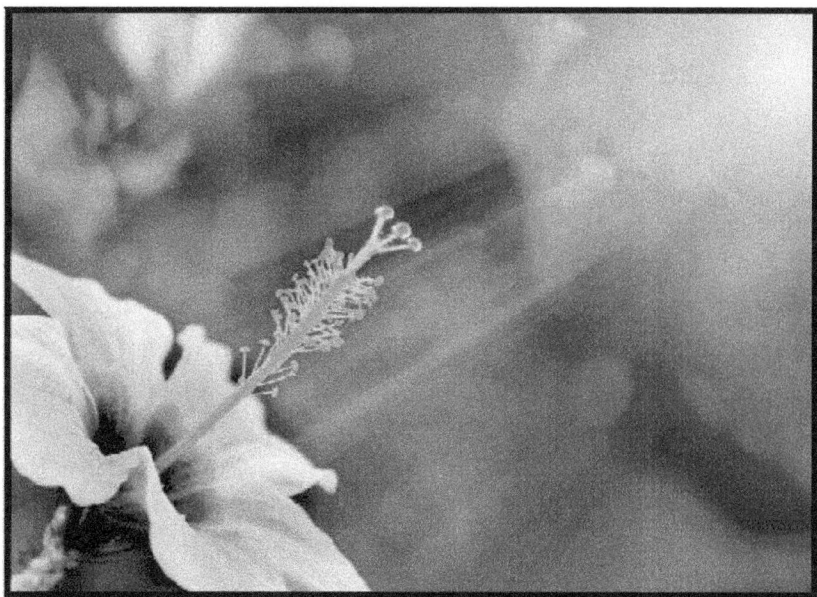

The sky isn't the limit; it's the starting line!

The Cleaning Meditation Visualization

Envision an island paradise surrounded by a wide, shallow river. Daily, you cross the river to your local town and back. The island paradise represents the realm of Source or the unconscious dream-state; the river water and riverbed represent the collective subconscious.

Along the way, you find various "deposits" on the riverbed left there by you and others. These represent memories. You and Source collaborate to clean-up and return the river to its natural, pristine state. We transmute these memories through repentance, forgiveness, gratitude, and love energies. By using the visualization, we take 100% responsibility and clean on specific issues without "engaging" or replaying the negative memories.

KEY: Go through all steps, even if only as a "witness."

It's easy to get stuck on the first and second steps; be mindful to keep moving forward and get that memory into super-consciousness' (Aumakua's) "hands." Once the Aumakua has the memory, he automatically moves the cleaning process through-to-completion. Time is irrelevant in terms of how long the process takes or where the memory exists in time-space (past, present, or future). Yes, that's right; you can clean the past, present, AND future! If you get interrupted mid-cleaning, it is equally effective to note where you left off and pick it up later.

The full Cleaning Meditation comprises 3 preparation steps and 4 cleaning steps (corresponding with repentance, forgiveness, gratitude, and love) for a total of 7-steps:

Step 1: Before you begin, summarize and name the issue (have fun, Unihipili loves this). This is the label for the energy that will be represented by an "icon" or symbol removed from the river. Resist the urge to get stuck in the memory and summarize it with a word, brief phrase, or simple image. **Try your best <u>not</u> to engage the memory any longer than it takes to name it**. Through this method, you can clean anything and everything, in your mind. The laws of physics are irrelevant in this mental space, and you have any superpower you can imagine. *The sky isn't the limit; it's the starting line!*

Step 2: In 1st or 3rd person, imagine walking through the river (Uhane). You are 100% safe, and the water is always perfect. Take a moment to envision immersing your whole body underwater and emerge refreshed and clean. This symbolizes the cleansing of everything, up to the instant of Now. The water washes away anything that could prevent you from feeling worthy and welcomed to perform this service with Source. Through the deep blue water, you see a vague outline of something that sank to the riverbed; and/or you gently bump into something with your foot. (This is the thing you want to clean that you named earlier).

<u>Step 3</u>: With that name or icon in-mind, reach into the water and lovingly lift the object that represents the word/icon out of the water. Your subconscious creates a mental image that embodies the energy you want to extract. It can be anything (any size, weight, texture, state of matter) you can imagine, as your subconscious will guide you. It need not match the name, but it can. If nothing comes up, make something up, or choose the first thing that comes to mind.

<u>Don't get stuck here</u> and ALWAYS focus on the word or icon, <u>NOT</u> the memory it represents. The only exception is to engage it ONLY to name it (and never again). The remaining steps match the 4-energies/phrases of the Ho'oponopono: *I'm Sorry (Repentance). Please Forgive Me (Forgiveness). Thank You (Gratitude). I Love You (Love).*

I'm Sorry   Please Forgive Me   Thank You   I Love You

I'm Sorry

I'm Sorry

Step 4: *Repentance*: After you lift the "object" out of the water (the bright light leaving the water in the illustration), examine it briefly and note its **basic** characteristics. Remember, nothing you pull out of the river can harm you, in any way. Regardless of what it is or who left it there, you're taking responsibility for cleaning the energy within you that is connected to the "object." I say "object" because it could be anything. I've pulled up a rusty truck engine, a ball of plasma, cities, aliens, galaxies, atoms, an ancient boat anchor, a cube of water vapor, bacteria, the Ark of The Covenant (that was insane), a pile of medieval weapons, armor the size of a planet, a toy car, etc. The "object" represents some aspect(s) of the energy you're cleaning. You can unpack the symbolic meanings **AFTER** the process is complete. Again, DO NOT analyze the "object" until after you complete the entire Cleaning Meditation.

You're saying, "I'm sorry" to Source (who created the pristine river and everything else), to Mother Earth, to yourself, and everyone/everything involved in this energy being "misplaced." Remember, it's from the "Collective Subconscious." And when you clean the part inside you, you clean the whole collective subconscious of the memory, permanently.

That's how Dr. Hew Len brought healing to an entire psych ward of criminals in a Hawaiian Mental Hospital using the Ho'oponopono. (That's right; he infused the entire hospital with Divine Love, through the Ho'oponopono, healing everyone). And he did this by meditating on the Ho'oponopono with each patient chart! He didn't have an official "therapy" session with any of the patients;

but he did spend time and interact with them regularly. He focused on the part of each patient's pain that's connected to energy within him. And there is **ZERO judgment** because, like Dr. Hew Len, the energies we clean in "others" also reside within us.

The anger that drives murder and violence, lust for power that drives sexual abuse, fears that drive paranoia, and much more lives within us all. As disturbing as this may be to accept, it's the "price" of gaining authority to clean it up. In my humble opinion, there is no greater honor than to be an "energetic servant" of all creation.

Warning: You may find a form of emotional or mental "amnesia" of the memories after cleaning. This is normal, if not welcomed by most. To be clear, one can NEVER clean all pain and negativity out of existence because it's part of existence. But, you can clean as much as possible and release the abundant power that was there all along.

Please Forgive Me

Please Forgive Me

Step 5: *Forgiveness*: Using your "Jedi" skills, levitate the "object" above your head. You're choosing to "let go," and give it to your Higher Self, the Aumakua. Once the object leaves your hands, your job is done! From this point forward, you simply "witness" the remaining steps. It **is** imperative that you "watch" the **entire** cleaning process happen in your mind's eye, each time. Aumakua is generous to forgive all parties involved. He's glad to remove this and everything related to the "deposit" from the river.

Remember, you're taking 100% responsibility for cleaning, NOT necessarily admitting fault unless that's appropriate. If appropriate, ask forgiveness from yourself, others, and Source for what you did. If you need to forgive anyone, you do so freely and generously!

In life, we encounter various forms of emotional "garbage" and disorder. We may have nothing to do with it being there; but we can be part of the solution to clean it up. Forgiveness is of vital significance. It must be practiced often to become a "natural reflex" to "deposits" in your river.

You can clean on other's behalf, especially if the situation involves you. And since you're working with Divine Love in the collective subconscious, it's a great way to bless those who've caused harm (Matthew 5:44 & Romans 12:14).

Thank You

Thank You

<u>Step 6</u>: *Gratitude*: Once the object is overhead, Aumakua (super-conscious/Higher Self) transforms it in some way (ornate gift wrapping, color changes, transmutation, etc.) and levitates it up to Source. It can go up "as-is" too. This step represents Aumakua (super-conscious) gathering everything related to it, throughout all time and space. This way, there's no need to think of everything related to the memory.

<u>Gratitude is plentiful here</u>: 1) gratitude towards the Aumakua and Source, 2) Aumakua and Source's gratitude towards you, 3) gratitude to and from the Universe, as all creation benefits from this cleaning. We can be confident in the full restoration of the memory since Source performs the actual cleaning and transmutation.

I Love You

<u>Step 7</u>: *Love*: When the "object" leaves Aumakua's "hands," it either explodes or implodes with a brilliant flash of pure light when it reaches Source. This occurs because Source is pure love and transmutes it instantly while creating something pristine in its place. Next, a beam of diamond-white or silver-gold light flows down, past the clouds, past the Aumakua, past the Uhane, all the way to the water (Unihipili) to fill the riverbed "hole" from which the energy came. Now, there is only pristine riverbed where the memory used to be.

This step represents the realignment of your Aumakua, Uhane, and Unihipili with Source. Congratulations, **you are now in a state of Pure Inspiration!** The "factory reset" and reintegration is complete. Love and gratitude overflow because Divine light represents pure Source energy: it's pure love for you and all Creation that's shines upon you and the ground on which you stand. You may remain in Inspiration until another memory knocks you out of alignment (happens to all of us in this dimension). When the meditation is complete, thank Source for the cleaning, knowing it's 100% finished.

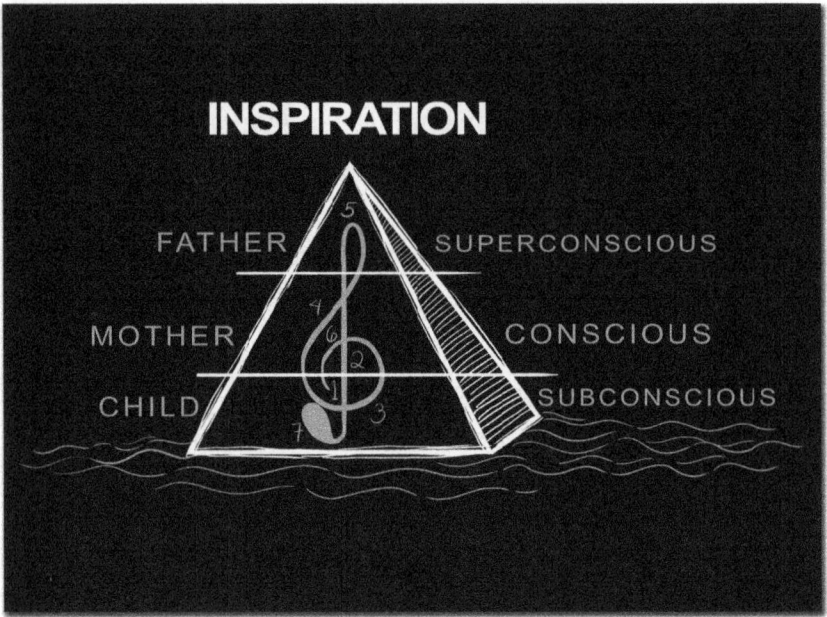

~~*

Source is infinite. Thus, it's impossible to clean "too often" from Source's perspective. Even if the totality of Creation's memory is cleaned, there will always be more to clean as new memories are created each passing moment. Since you're working with Source towards a common goal, cleaning strengthens your relationship with Source and your love for all creation.

> "The purpose of life is to be restored back to Love, moment to moment. To fulfill this purpose, the individual must acknowledge that he is 100 percent responsible for creating his life the way it is. He must come to see that it is his thoughts that create his life the way it is, moment to moment. The problems are not people, places, and situations but rather the thoughts of them." -Dr. Ihaleakala Hew Len

Dr. Hew Len's quote summarizes why The Cleaning Meditation is vital to rebuild and strengthen your marriage. Your wife is NOT the problem; it's your thoughts about her, and vice-versa. If the same issue appears to "return" to your awareness, simply clean it again until it integrates or passes out of your life. However, it's best not to clean on the identical issue too often or obsess because you're engaging the memory. Engaging the memory is counterproductive because you're GIVING the memory energy with your attention (amplification). But if intuition prompts you to clean again, do it!

Throughout the process, it's important to feel emotions and sensations as much as possible. Allow love, gratitude, forgiveness, and repentance to permeate your being. There is no rush here. Remember, time is an illusion. Forgive all people, places, and things. Everything is consciousness, so even particles, places, and objects can hold memories.

Clean as often as required. Source is always grateful and happy to see you in-general and when performing this cleaning. Pause: Meditate on that idea right now. God is happy to see you!

Many generations will thank you for what you're doing here-and-now. Cleaning removes the emotional charge from memories, releasing their grip on your subconscious. Simultaneously, the painful memory is removed from Shadow's "torture tool bag." This clears many blocks to your connections with yourself, Source, and others.

Why remove emotional charges from memories? The emotional charge is how Shadow triggers your negative memories. In our brains, the amygdala responds to situations based on similar events from the past. It does this to determine if you are in mortal danger or not. Often emotions are felt before the conscious thoughts that triggered them. When you have negative emotions about a past situation, he can link that awful memory to any number of present and future situations. By removing the emotional charge, you break the cycle.

Dr. Hew Len once said, "you either live in a state of memory or inspiration." This is not simply a deep esoteric commentary on consciousness; **it's an instruction:** Live in Inspiration! That's where your desires come to fruition, dreams are fulfilled, and your environment becomes the fullness of everyone's highest good.

The Cleaning Meditation Illustration

Cleaning Meditation FAQ

Q: How often should I do this?

A: As often as practical! This is internal work that can be done anytime, anywhere (as long as you're safe). Like everything in life, this can get out of balance and become excessive; sometimes you need to clean on the Cleaning Meditation for proper integration into your healthy lifestyle. Often you need to take a break from cleaning and enjoy life, as is. Be careful not to obsess over cleaning (to my fellow OCD folks out there!)

Q: What if the issue "returns" or appears unchanged?

A: Continue cleaning until it *integrates* or *dissipates*.

- *Integration*: it becomes part of you through acceptance and love with no further negative charge towards it.
- *Dissipation*: it moves downstream and out of your life.

Disconnection perpetuates pain. Integration heals. Think of <u>Neo & Smith</u> (The Matrix), <u>Flynn & CLU</u> (Tron: Legacy), <u>Luke & Vader</u> (Star Wars: Return Of The Jedi), and <u>Yoda vs. Dark Yoda</u> (Star Wars: Clone Wars). Integration and dissipation occur through transmutation. Transmutation means <u>transforming</u> one thing into another.

Remember, there are only two mental states: **Memory** or **Inspiration**. If a memory appears to return, it is seldom the exact one you've already cleaned, unless:

1) You didn't get to the root of the issue (Incomplete Cleaning)

2) Your energy and intentions were impure (Inaccurate Cleaning)

3) It's resolved for you, but others involved are still learning (In-Progress Cleaning)

4) Source resolved the energies but allowed you to "weather the storm" for a higher purpose (Instructional Cleaning)

5) You have more cleaning to do, acceptance to attain, or a mystery to uncover that involves the memory and your life's mission. (Integration Cleaning)

Regarding #5 above (and the "I.C." explanations), you may have merely "scratched the surface" of a larger issue. But I caution you about obsessing; just clean and move on. Intuition will inform your next steps as you meditate.

When there is a specific person that you want out of your life, besides cleaning, the most effective approach (that causes the least harm) is to "love them <u>out</u> of your life." What does that mean? It means love them! Serve them. Be kind, compassionate, and forgiving. If the person means you harm, your kindness will repel them. Therefore, you stop the cycle of pain in a way that brings healing to you both.

Q: What types of effects should I expect?

A: The effects usually happen in stages; some are immediate, and others take time to manifest. In terms of immediate effects, the meditation is calming, freeing, and empowering. After doing this meditation for many years, I still feel effects immediately and throughout the meditation. Yet, sometimes I don't feel much. Either way, the meditation is equally effective.

Please understand that this will "shake things up" in your world because you're impacting the collective subconscious. You're often undoing Shadow's work. I've become accustomed to seeing the unexpected in people and situations. But it ALWAYS works out for the best.

If things appear to "get worse" after performing the meditation, that's confirmation that IT IS WORKING! As in the physical world, cleaning often makes a bigger mess in the beginning while you clear away the "initial mess" to reach the "main mess" that needs to be cleaned. It's like clearing out a basement or attic. Throughout the process, the mess worsens as we move things around. Dust is kicked up. Dirt is tracked through the house, etc.

The effects of the Cleaning Meditation vary from minds and hearts being changed, situations beginning or ending, healing of self and others, gaining wisdom and insights, finding solutions, problems decrease, or problems increase for a season then move out of your life. I can say with absolute certainty, I have yet to experience a lack of impact. Something always changes, transforms, moves, stays in place (while everything else moves), arrives, departs, or some other psychological, physical, emotional, and/or spiritual benefit. Often, when nothing appears to change, it is YOU that's changed. Sometimes, the solution to a conflict is to change YOUR heart on the issue.

When you're in the middle of a storm praying for it to stop, sometimes the solution is that Source guides you out or fortifies your position to ride it out. That means you either go *through* the storm or weather the storm (Guide-out or Ride-out). Why? The storm may serve a higher purpose for you and others, which requires it to continue. Other times, the storm will cease or you're delivered from it. Remember, life isn't <u>all</u> about you or <u>all</u> about others. Either way, this meditation will yield the best results (highest good) for all involved when used with love. After cleaning, be vigilant and look for anything that has changed in the people, places, and/or things related to the transformed energy.

Regarding depression, we mustn't be against medication, psychiatry, psychologists, and/or therapists. Just as an orthopedic cast holds broken bones in place to heal properly, proper meds and therapy can help. I'm a huge proponent of "throwing everything we have" (<u>including the kitchen sink</u>) at challenges, including medicine, modern science, ancient wisdom, and spirituality.

Sometimes Source doesn't heal an ailment immediately because the self-healing process is already underway. As cuts heal after being cleaned and bandaged, our immune system and many other body systems facilitate constant healing.

The Cleaning Meditation can be used with current medication(s) and therapies until such time they are no longer necessary (TBD by your healthcare team). This meditation has no known contraindications with any medication or therapy.

IMPORTANT: DO NOT expect to levitate or walk on water after meditating. It doesn't work that way. The bottom line is that when you change your "internal" energy about the "external" world, you change the world.

Q: Why was this meditation developed?

A: One of the core tenants of the SITH class is "non-engagement of memories." You "engage" a memory when you give it your attention, replay it in your mind, or discuss it. This presents a major challenge: how do you clean memories without

ENGAGING MEMORIES

It happens subconsciously. We just find ourselves in various life situations, with negative memories playing across our minds. This incites anxiety, fear, rage, etc...Either Shadow initiates this, or you're stuck in a thought loop/pattern. Break-free through Inspiration!

engaging them? And if you try not to engage them, you're engaging them! It's like saying "clean up that pile of poop, but don't think about the pink elephants that made it." It's a funny mental picture isn't it (I mean, is their poop pink too)!?

The solution arrived during meditation when I considered that the subconscious speaks in images, symbols, and various mental/emotional impressions. For simplicity, I've labeled this "the language of the subconscious."

By using symbols to represent the memories and energy, we can clean with specificity and intention without engaging the memory. We can take 100% responsibility for what happened, process the appropriate emotions, and enjoy repentance. You receive all the benefits of cleaning, without replaying the memories in your mind (i.e. no "pink poop")!

With Source's connection to the collective subconscious (Unihipili) and Super-conscious (Aumakua), The Cleaning Meditation facilitates our choice to infuse love with our waking consciousness (Uhane). After pulling something out of the water, the Aumakua "packages" or transforms the object. Again, this symbolizes the Super-conscious' gathering of all related energies throughout all time, space, dimensions, scales, etc. This also ensures the "subconscious icon" is always in the proper form for Source to accept.

The blinding light of Source represents the final transmutation of the object into its pristine form. The light that fills the "hole" in the riverbed represents Source's completion of the final transmutation and integration process. I also like to think of it as Source "beaming down" a pristine replacement (shameless Trekkie reference)!

The Cleaning Meditation is an original creation through Inspiration in 2013 based on principles from EC, Ho'oponopono, and tremendous trial and error followed by error, error, and more error...with another "trial" or two in there. The coherence breathing exercise (based on the InnerSmile and HeartMath) promotes self-healing, longevity, intuition, positive moods, and a host of other benefits. By marrying these, Cleaning becomes a potent method for self-discovery, healing, and reconciliation.

With the support of a fellow EC and friend Darek Laviolette (retired Navy S.E.A.L. trainer), we worked through integrating the Ho'oponopono concepts into our lives. As Derek and I wrestled with the non-engagement of memories, Inspiration gave me the vision that became the process we used every day, for over one year straight.

Darek and I cleaned everything we could imagine in this universe and beyond. Having traveled the planet and seen the unspeakable, Darek and I had our hands-full cleaning based on his various tours-of-duty. For me, it was overwhelming and a relentless mirror of all the horrific to angelic energies within the collective subconscious. It was cathartic and deeply healing for both of us, as I healed a lot within myself in the process. Then Darek put me in his "crosshairs" for healing and walked me, step-by-step, out of the pit of suicidal depression. He challenged me to not just make things go away, but take action to repair and make amends (like repaying all my debt by 2020). His mental toughness, focus, and dedication poured the foundation for the Cleaning Meditation (more about Darek under Next Steps: Ground Rules).

Q: What's a more scientific explanation of Cleaning?

A: Ok, for all you "woo woo" haters, physics shows that everything is light and information (AKA "data"). Data is expressed, fundamentally, in the spin and position of various common particles. Photons are light and information in a vibratory form (spinning).

All sensory information is data processed by the brain, and our subconscious can process around 400 billion bits per second. In comparison, our conscious mind can only process a mere 2,000 bits per second! That leaves tremendous data to be processed by the subconscious.

We choose (as an act of will) to "engage" or "disengage" thoughts/memories that flow down the river of consciousness. But we seldom address the "emotional baggage."

The emotional charge is the "default" or "programmed" feeling response based on the memory. As thoughts and memories flow like a river, you aren't in control of the speed or direction of flow (ask any white-water rafter). But you can adjust your position (navigate) by choosing where you focus your attention.

Memories are stored data. Like deleting files and emptying the "Recycle Bin" on your computer, you can rewrite and remove memories from your subconscious that recreate undesired emotions. On computers, system resources remain impacted by 'deleted" files until you empty the "Recycle Bin."

Subconscious recreations are the root of tremendous suffering, on all levels. To alleviate suffering, we must remove the emotional charge and meaning(s) associated with the memory. The Cleaning Meditation facilitates that process.

It's like defective computer hardware or software that's returned to the manufacturer. Our job is to release memories (from the Unihipili via the Uhane) for Aumakua to deliver to Source (like a spiritual "mail carrier").

Remember, when you're envisioning the past, you are engaging those memories. This activates the primitive parts of our <u>brains</u> characterized by amygdala-driven responses, causing unbridled emotion and disconnection from self and others. This is where the "fight-or-flight" reflex is triggered, which has very real physiological and psychological effects. It keeps you stuck in patterns, preventing you from experiencing what's next. But wait, there's more!

Carl Jung wrote about "the collective subconscious" and Rupert Sheldrake postulates the existence of "<u>morphic resonance fields</u>." These match the Ho'oponopono concepts about the super-conscious and subconscious being linked to a greater source. Indeed, science is coming into alignment with spiritual traditions more and more each day!

This meditation is the synthesis of ancient and modern spiritual traditions. Ho'oponopono ideas have parallels in Ancient Kemet (Egypt) with the brain structures that were represented by certain "neters." LP is an attempt to bridge the gap between science, philosophy, and spirituality just as many Ancient cultures all over the world accomplished millennia before us.

Where's the evidence for that claim? Well, there are only a few thousand across the globe (Angkor Wat, countless sites throughout India, all the Pyramids of Egypt, Teotihuacan in Mexico, and Stonehenge to Antarctica). Since many sites are megalithic, one could say there's a sizeable amount of evidence!

That tangent was relevant to show that there was much more knowledge in antiquity than previously thought. Within the last few centuries, we've just started to "catch up." We're just now making discoveries that were etched in stone thousands of years ago.

Q: What differs between the Ho'oponopono and LP?

A: Shadow. In the SITH class (Ho'oponopono), there was little discussion about the dark-side or how to address it. Negativity was merely a self-evident cause for cleaning. However, this difference unlocks the power of both methods. When you understand how Shadow works and apply Ho'oponopono to clean up his messes, he doesn't stand a chance!

I recommend reading Dr. Hew Len's "Who's in Charge?" document on the SITH website whenever you're ready. NOTE: The connected pyramid in his illustrations is the state of Inspiration. The disconnected pyramid = engaging a memory.

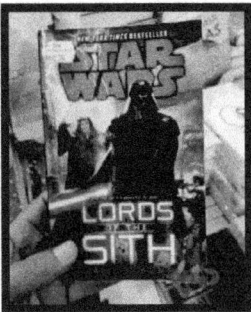

BTW: For all the Star Wars fans that are uncomfortable with the term "SITH," have no fear because I consider myself a Grey Jedi! By choosing love, you're already on the light side. And Ho'oponopono is ALSO the path of the "light-side" of The Force. The SITH program is administered by lovely individuals who are well aware of the name issue, and they clean on it regularly. Remember, Void is Source NOT darkness. Light and dark come from Void. But I digress.

Q: What influence does Shadow have on cleaning?

A: Shadow and his cronies HATE cleaning with every fiber of their being. However, they are powerless to impact the process anymore than darkness can impact bright light. With that in mind, Shadow can <u>attempt</u> to:

1) Distract you from starting, maintaining, or completing the cleaning process.
2) Cloud your mind to prevent you from discovering the root of an issue.
3) Fill you with guilt, condemnation, shame, self-loathing, worry, etc. to paralyze you.
4) Frighten you and others away (with no real ability to deliver on his threats).
5) Thwart your efforts with some yet-to-be discovered dark tactic.

It's imperative to remember he's just a shadow! Like a barking miniature-dog with no claws or teeth, he can cause a ruckus but no real damage (in comparison to a human). However, this "mini-dog" inflicts harm by inciting nearby humans to do real damage to each other.

At his worst, he is only the "**<u>shadow of death</u>**," **<u>NOT</u>** the Angel of death (<u>Psalm 23:4</u>).

Q: What if I don't believe in a "higher power"?

A: A wise man once answered: "Ask me that when you're on your deathbed." In one way or another, nearly everyone believes in a higher power, be it energy, God, science, the Milky Way, your "future self," or even observations made by your senses. Since our concept of reality is formed from various "electrical signals interpreted by the brain," even our senses require an element of faith. Who's to say our senses detect what's "real" at all? What if we're tethered to a cosmic energy grid within "fluidic space" that Shadow commandeers to drain our life force while projecting an immersive holographic simulation?

In today's world, science has become the de facto "god" with many devotees that spread arrogance and spiritual detachment. Why do I say this? Let's imagine, for a moment, you are a sentient, self-aware quantum software program running within a simulation. To think one can understand how the simulated universe works from within is as asinine as trying to fathom the inner workings of a laptop as a single bit of information on one layer of software running on it. Who's to say this "reality" isn't merely one of countless running on the same system? Even if you could understand how a hard drive, RAM, GPU, CPU, motherboard, peripherals, power supply, drivers, OS, and software work by reverse-engineering the Simulation, you would still have to answer this question: "who built the damn thing, programmed the simulation, and why?"

As Morpheus said to Neo before he took the red pill, "Unfortunately, no one can be told what the Matrix is; you have to see it for yourself." Using this Matrix movie analogy, how could anyone within The Matrix know they're in a liquid-filled pod in a "machine field" while jacked-in to the Matrix? How could they know or believe that when they "die" in the Matrix, they're being picked like cotton to power the machine world and used up like a battery? Within the Matrix, even programs knew that the Oracle and Architect exist (venerable and veritable "higher powers"). You can only understand the hardware and the simulation from outside of it (as in "The Matrix" movie).

In our mind's eye and heart, we can connect with an infinite Source. Science demonstrates the impacts of meditation on physiology and psychology. The mind triggers the same physiological reactions with actual **and** imagined situations. Even if you think it's all "imaginary," your brain and body respond as if it's real; and I submit that it **IS** real.

As I said at the beginning of this book, suspend judgment and at least do a "thought experiment" that "Source Consciousness" exists. With Source included in your worldview, what are the implications for you and the billions of other people around the world who believe in some form of God? The bottom line is that The Cleaning Meditation works, even from a purely psychological and scientific standpoint.

Q: Is there an underlying scientific basis for any of this?

A: Psychology Today wrote an excellent article on the Ho'oponopono and the practice of radical responsibility. It's a purely academic article written through the lens of psychological research.

Modern physicists point to the existence of micro-singularities in protons. These theories assert that everything came forth from these singularities (Void). These theories suggest that Void preceded the "Big Bang." This supports the theory of the holographic universe, as the proton micro-singularities match the black holes that we find at the center of galaxies. A singularity or black hole is void.

Sacred geometry is comprised of recurring mathematical constants, ratios, shapes, etc. that pervade nature from the microscopic to the macroscopic. This matches Gnostic writings that allude to a sacred "spiral pattern" used to contain the profuse spilling forth of life from Void. We know this as the "Golden Spiral."

Everything in nature points to intelligent design. I'm merely assigning an Identity to the "Intelligent Designer" called Source (or God).

The double-slit experiments show that consciousness is connected to everything. Quantum Physics demonstrates, mathematically, everything is connected via a common substrate (Quantum Foam, the Hindu "Milky Ocean", Zero Point Energy, Source, Space-Time, etc.).

Computers provide excellent models to help us understand reality. In most operating systems, desktop icons represent complex instructions that interface with multiple system layers to perform specific tasks. The program will not execute unless you run it or schedule it to run at a future time. In the Cleaning Meditation, the subconscious object we lift from the water represents every aspect of the situation, just as an Icon represents an entire software program on a computer. With this analogy, I think of cleaning as "uninstalling and updating" our mental/spiritual "software."

The HeartMath Institute has done extensive research on the human bio-energy field illustrating the profound influence our heart has on ourselves and our surroundings. This lends credence to the importance of energy in our lives. By focusing our intention on love and compassion, we positively impact the Universe on every level. Though, in my humble opinion, the Ho'oponopono needs no scientific explanations. The results speak for themselves. Dr. Hew Len's work at the Hawaii Mental Hospital and countless examples in my life are all the evidence I need.

Lastly ("extra credit" for all my "over-achievers" out there), Blue Solar Water is recommended throughout the Ho'oponopono class for cleaning. It's water in a blue glass bottle that's left out in the Sun to absorb its energy (approx. one hour). This is mentioned in Dr. Hew Len's "Who's In Charge" paper. Recently, Solar Water has been demonstrated scientifically via research on a new state of matter for water. Remember, the adult human body and our planet consists of approximately 70% water. If healing energy can be infused into water, how much more can energy influence other aspects of our life? Also, Dr. Emoto's Nobel Prize-winning experiments show the profound impact of thoughts, words, and intentions on water molecules. Everything is connected!

Q: What's a non-spiritual explanation for why it works?

A: Energy psychology is a fast-emerging field. The Cleaning Meditation is a powerful form of Energy Psychology. We work directly with the subconscious, conscious, and super-conscious minds through the Cleaning Meditation. The process helps us identify and resolve emotional attachments to subconscious memories that impact our lives.

The Cleaning Meditation gives the "wandering mind" a clear focus and intention. Just as journaling "tricks" the brain into thinking you've been "heard," Cleaning helps your mind release the emotional charge associated with subconscious memories, with minimal resistance.

As you focus on repentance (changing your ways, for the better), forgiveness (releasing negative feelings associated with a person, place, or thing), gratitude (appreciating something/someone), and love (connection), your mind remains focused and engaged. You may even feel positive emotions for an extended time after cleaning, which benefits the body and mind in countless ways.

Forgiveness and love come from the heart, yet the mind comprehends and interprets them. The Cleaning Meditation impacts both in profound ways. I will obtain more scientific data on this technique soon; but tremendous research already exists on the benefits of meditation, brainwave entrainment, hypnotherapy, affirmations, compassion, positive mental imagery, and more.

NEXT STEPS

LP Mastery

Think of LP as one of those "rolling tool cabinets" you see in an auto mechanic's garage. You don't use all of your tools for each job, but you have the tools you need for each job. The goal is to become adept at the techniques that resonate most with you. Then, you can reach the ultimate level of becoming an "official" Love Provider "Self-Coach." This is a position of honor and distinction, and a prerequisite to becoming an actual LP Coach. A LP Self-Coach is the embodiment of the axiom "physician, heal thyself."

When you make mistakes, fall short, have a moment of weakness (as we all do), go back and analyze the interaction considering <u>your side</u> of the conversation from a 3rd Person perspective (what you did, said, felt, intended, etc). Look at *yourself* as a LP client. What would you say to your past-self from an LP perspective, based on what you know now?

This is mastery through teaching one's self. And teaching is how you become a master! Who better to teach **you** than you!? Why wait for a coach, mentor, or therapist when you can find all the answers and insights you need in the nearest mirror? And if you **do** talk with a 3rd party for help, <u>you'll have clarity and insight to **help them help you**</u>.

As I said in the beginning, a coach can help and support, but you're the one who has to play the game. Star athletes don't expect the coach to play the game for them or give them ALL the answers, right? Most athletes WANT to play the game! And answers are often found by "walking the path."

Review the "Confirmation Subroutine" and "Ask Yourself Great Questions" sections of the forthcoming "LP Action Guide" for your "self-coaching practice." Remember, my goal is self-sufficiency. This is where it happens. I want you to benefit from this comprehensive array of tools to be a "Jack-of-all-trades" AND a Master of One as a Love Provider!

If you need additional guidance, support, or a swift kick in the rear, see below for more information on LP Coaching:

This is YOUR hero story!

Love Provider Coaching Structure

1. Questionnaire
2. Love Provider Book
3. Scheduled Video Conferences or Phone Calls. 1-on-1 or Group.

Two Paths. One Program: **Reconnection / Refinement**

- **Reconnection**: Clearly, you had a connection, or you wouldn't have gotten married; we need to re-establish and strengthen it. Reconciliation naturally follows reconnection.

- **Refinement**: Improve your existing marriage and hone key skills to sustain it.

Love Provider Mission:

Love Provider mastery entails empowerment and tremendous personal growth through <u>100% responsibility</u>. We'll use the methods I used in my reconciliation and rebuilding process. Backed by science and years of practical application, you'll apply The Cleaning Meditation to clean-up your destructive subconscious programs and live a powerful, connected life of inspiration.

A strong commitment is required to complete the program. Even if you finish early or choose to stop, please schedule a final call to close the loop. The final call is an opportunity to celebrate achievements, recap what was learned, ensure you're set up for success and improve the program to help more marriages succeed. You have to see-it-through to receive all the benefits. This is YOUR hero story.

This program differs from many other treatments or therapies, as the goal is true self-sufficiency. As the adage says, 'give a man a fish, he eats for a day; teach a man to fish, he eats for a lifetime." I designed this program to "teach you how to fish" within the infinite river of consciousness. As such, there are no "career-students" allowed. If you follow the program "to the letter" without finding success, perhaps this is not the program for you; and I WANT you to move on to find something that works for you. My only desire is to see more marriages succeed.

We may or may not reach <u>all</u> of your goals before completing the program; that's okay because that's not the point. The point **IS** the process. Once you know you can achieve your goals through the process, you can apply it to achieve anything you want.

The point IS the process.

Do unto <u>yourself</u> as you would have others do unto you.

Love Provider Orientation

How It Works:

I'll provide concepts and insights, tips and tricks, questions and answers, accountability and support, and share wisdom gleaned from 7 years of rebuilding my marriage and living the LP lifestyle. Everything I share was refined in the crucible of my marriage and validated by other's success in applying the same principles. Today, Gina is my best friend, life-partner, lover, girlfriend, and wife, while being a fantastic mother to our three children and multiple "fur babies" (AKA pets). We go on regular dates and genuinely enjoy each other's company. This is significant because we spent our first 11+ years together being miserable or separated. My brilliant and lovely wife inspired much of this program through insights from her perspective.

You'll receive zero judgment from me; if I did, I would only judge myself. I've made a metric ton of mistakes (and still do) and learn from each one. However, the harsh truth is that it's an "emotional addiction" or an addiction to feeling a particular way, even if it's unpleasant.

Why? The same nerve receptors that respond to chemical compounds in cocaine and heroin also respond to the neurotransmitters associated with emotions. And, many visceral sensations are indistinguishable from the emotions they compliment. For instance, the sensation of fear and excitement are nearly identical, other than the meaning we assign to it. Tears of sorrow and joy physically feel the same. The feeling of anxiety and asphyxiation are very similar (So, BREATHE).

As with most drugs, you build up a tolerance and begin to crave it. Simultaneously, your subconscious gets attached to this habit, and you continue to create situations to elicit that emotion (usually unintentionally). Unless you reprogram your subconscious to create new possibilities, you'll continue on this proverbial hamster wheel, going nowhere. That's why the "grass is **not** greener" in other relationships. You merely transfer your addiction to the next person.

To break an emotional addiction, you need to replace it with something else. It's **so** easy to beat up on yourself, be self-critical, and self-deprecating. Instead, I propose that you "do unto yourself as you would have others do unto you." I call this the "Diamond Rule." The "Diamond Rule" is about treating **yourself** with compassion, kindness, patience, love, and forgiveness that you desire and give to others. It means using the power of your words to speak life unto yourself! If we say "Love Providers share kindness with everyone," **YOU'RE** included in "everyone."

Often, we treat others with such love, gentleness, patience, kindness, forgiveness, etc. and it's genuine! We give the "benefit of the doubt" to others and give people multiple chances after making mistakes. But with ourselves, we're harsh, critical, demeaning, shaming, unforgiving, impatient, vindictive, hateful, and we wonder why we're ill and depressed all the time!

With self-respect and self-worth, you love yourself and cultivate positive thoughts about that amazing, good-looking person in the mirror. In turn, others respect, value, and think highly of you because they're mirroring your internal state back to you. Since the external world is a mirror of what's inside you, cultivate internal love, compassion, and gratitude for self so THAT is reflected instead!

Forgive Yourself.

Ground Rules

Be kind, patient, and forgive <u>yourself</u> always (Diamond Rule). We all make mistakes and we did the best we could at the time, with what we knew. Now we're learning better ways; as a result, we must focus on being present and moving forward, while learning from the past. Shadow will gladly beat you to a pulp by himself. There's no need to do his job for him!

Take notes during sessions or soon after. It will help you recall what you learned (even if recorded). Everyone will have to push boundaries and leave their comfort zone. I did, you will too. Exploration and discovery require a departure from the status quo. But the journey can be easier with key skills and *"proper preparation"* (try to say that 5X fast).

Suspend judgment and give these techniques your 100% best efforts, for an extended timeframe (3-6 months). This is the only way to see real change and find your truth. Like working out at a gym, you won't see results until you build muscle and endurance through *consistent effort over time*.

Be 100% open and honest in your sessions. Your LP Coach will be honest with you, and they ask the same in return. Your coaching time is brief. While we're happy to listen to "he-said-she-said" (if that's truly what you need), that is not the best use of your time or ours. The other benefit is that honesty shortens your learning curve, substantially.

Everything said during each session is strictly confidential. Your coach **may** discuss an anonymous summary of outcomes with program leadership (with your consent), but only to best support you. If there's something you'd like to keep confidential (within the confines of the law), tell your coach immediately. Please understand that threats to harm yourself or others will be taken seriously. Remember, these sessions are for **you**, and you alone. If you share insights from your sessions with others, be sure to encourage them to book their own session!

I've mentioned 100% often throughout this program. That's because 100% is expected and required to gain LP Mastery. I gleaned this standard from elite military veterans. The Navy S.E.A.L.s won't tolerate half-ass efforts, and neither will I. I had the distinct privilege of working with a retired Navy S.E.A.L. trainer named Darek Laviolette (via phone, text, and Skype) every day for over one year. He took the Ho'oponopono class (at a different location) a month before me. I have him to thank for getting me through some of the darkest times of my reconciliation and literally "talking me off the ledge" multiple times. Reconciling and rebuilding my marriage was one of the most challenging things I have ever done. I know I survived the process through Derek's help (much love and respect my friend).

Additionally for over a year, I've had the honor and privilege of being mentored by a professional preacher with a Doctorate in Ministry and multiple Master's degrees. He's a retired Marine Force Recon Sniper, master martial artist, prolific bible scholar, and engineer for one of the largest privately owned data centers on Earth. He's a great man and great friend known as "the RightRevRhino," Dr. Elder Pastor A.J. Watkins (I just call him "Pastor AJ"). From tremendous biblical wisdom and knowledge of sacred texts to practical relationship advice, Pastor AJ provided the final pieces of the puzzle I've been assembling for the past 30 years! He helped me rediscover the suppressed "Alpha Male" within me. His anointing, brutal honesty, and world-class spiritual knowledge kept me on the straight-and-narrow like a 12lb ball in bumper bowling!

The unwavering accountability and support of these true heroes and highly respected friends made all this possible. Without them, Gina and I would be divorced. In fact, I would likely be dead if not for their strength and character. It's what motivated me to become a relationship coach. As a man who's made it to the other side, it's **so** worth it! And I wouldn't trade a moment of pain to get here! That's saying a lot.

•-• Rx •-•

<u>Research</u> shows that it takes substantially more than 21 days to form a new habit (probably closer to 90 days). To develop new habits, we need to change how you feel and break the emotional addiction.

To change how you feel, change your thoughts. To change your thoughts, change your awareness. And we expand awareness with knowledge confirmed through experience.

The program is structured for 7-sessions. As such, I can work within fewer sessions, but we'll only cover a portion of the material. This Rx has the side effect of properly setting you up for success. The best-case scenario is 5-7 sessions. This provides time to dive deep into each principle and provide custom insights for your unique situation.

Sessions are one hour (1-on-1) or 90-Minutes for Group Sessions. It's ideal to wait at least 1-2 weeks between sessions to allow time for practical application. That's why sessions are no more often than bi-monthly.

- Session 1 & 2: Establish new habits and goals.
- Session 3: Mid-Point Review & Next Steps.
- Session 4 & 5: Work through the next new habit/goal.
- Session 6: Final check and clarification of your path.
- Session 7: Wrap-up and set you up for continued success.

In the final session, we'll review what you learned, discuss what worked or didn't work, and determine the next steps. In this way, you can be a part of helping more people enjoy great marriages by improving the program! We're here to help in any way we can. And we're your ally and biggest fan of your success!

It's time to reclaim your power! Here's a little shift in perspective: did Shadow create your problems, or did you? The answer is **_YOU_**. Shadow has <u>no</u> power to create anything alone. He can only manipulate you to create what **he wants**. You have <u>all</u> the power. Shadow did not manifest your issues alone. He manipulated you and your wife to manifest problems with <u>your</u> power.

When you expand yourself, you can no longer remain contained within the same mental prison. Your consciousness is powerful; it always has been and always will be. What else would you expect as a child of the Creator? When you remember this truth, you will no longer agree to stay confined.

One of Shadow's oldest tricks is to make you believe you're powerless next to him. Shadow **is** the fence in your prison, but your heart is the gate. The only way he can control you is to put you in a smaller box than he is in. Reconnect with what you know is right, at your core, to rise above and break free.

Martin Luther King said, "Cowardice asks the question, is it safe? Expediency asks the question, is it politic? Vanity asks the question, is it popular? But conscience asks the question, is it right? And there comes a time when one must take a position that is neither safe, nor politic, nor popular; but one must take it because it's right." We are consciousness, pure awareness. And intuitively, we know what's right. Your intuition or higher-self is all-knowing (especially compared to us). When we reconnect with intuition, we know what's right as a matter of conscience.

There is such a glorious life on the other side of 100% responsibility. Though it's a challenging path, it changes you from the inside-out with each step. Don't just do this for your wife or even your kids, do it to be the best version of **you** possible! Isn't that the greatest gift you could give your family and the world?

The most powerful sculpture of Burning Man 2015 depicts two adults with their backs to each other after a disagreement; meanwhile, their "inner child" just wants to connect. The sculpture is entitled "Love" created by Ukrainian artist Alexander Milov. Whenever you're upset with your wife, remember "Love."

Photo Courtesy of: Gerome Viavant

Make It Your Reality!

One of the best decisions I made in my life was marrying my wife, Gina. The second best decision was to do whatever it took to keep her. It's true that, from the perspective of higher dimensions, time is irrelevant; however, I ***implore you*** not to waste the precious time we have in this "glove box" reality.

Through all of my crazy life experiences, I **know** our souls live forever, in one form or another. From the perspective of eternity, our time here on Earth is but a single droplet of mist in the brisk morning air at sunrise. But let's bring this back down to Earth, back to this moment, right here, right now.

Let's consider how precious our time is here. Every moment is a gift (even the painful ones). Why shouldn't we spend it doing the things we love with those we love the most? It's **not** something only a select few enjoy. We're infinite in awareness, and we <u>can all</u> experience the best life has to offer. There's MORE than enough to go around if we work together through harmony and cooperation.

I'll close with this <u>profound video about our time on Earth</u>. May you savor each moment while growing evermore connected to Source. I wish you days filled with peace, harmony, compassion, and joy illuminated by love. Indeed, love is the most powerful creative and healing force in the universe.

I hope and pray that you found something helpful within these pages, and I wish you even greater success than you can imagine!

May you create the marriage of **your** dreams right now in your imagination and use the power of Love to make it your reality!

...

Wait. . .for. . .it... :)

...

How do I become, based on a Love Supreme, 'a force for good'...

Okay...FINAL thoughts:

To the Reader: Thank you so much for sticking with this and allowing me to share these ideas with you. I want to be clear that I'm **not** suggesting anyone believes anything in particular. I'm just sharing my puzzle pieces to see if they fit with yours. Maybe you'll suggest that I invert a piece or rotate it, but I know the pieces all form the same picture. And each piece is required to form the complete picture.

The spiritual concepts and principles are where the power resides in the Cleaning Meditation. When you apply an expanded awareness to this meditation, the miraculous becomes commonplace. Things work out for the best, by default, and you spend most of your time trying to decide how to bless others with your abundance. And the best way to bless others is to be the blessing!

Like emergency oxygen masks on airlines, we're instructed to put our mask on <u>first</u> before helping others. We need to fill ourselves with love, joy, and compassion until it overflows onto everyone around us! We'll <u>never</u> run out of resources nor need anything from anyone because we're fulfilled by Source. This principle has changed my life, in countless positive ways. And genuinely, I want to share as much positivity with as many people as possible.

Concepts were explained from a spiritual, philosophical, scientific, biological, logical, historical, and comical standpoint to speak to a multitude of people. Regardless of your faith, spiritual tradition, or scientific view of Reality, I hope you've gleaned something to improve your life in some way. If nothing else, this represents different perspectives on many topics!

Thank you for your patience and openness to my unique thoughts on spirituality and metaphysical concepts. Though I do not subscribe to any particular religion, I lean towards Christianity, Gnosticism, and Buddhism. But I love many Hindu beliefs, ancient Egyptian spiritual traditions, and many others I've studied on my journey.

To be clear, I have **zero interest** in starting a religion or Church. I want to free minds, like Morpheus in The Matrix. And this can be accomplished within most religious and spiritual traditions. I believe this is possible because they all, ultimately, come from the same Source.

If this book did not resonate with you, please gift it to someone.

The more lives are enriched, the more successful, joyful, and fulfilling marriages can flourish. Though problems are part of life, if the positives outweigh the negatives, you're winning! I want people to enjoy life rather than suffer through it. And if the individuals suffer, the marriage suffers.

Marriage can be **SO** gratifying. But it takes mutual respect, regular maintenance, self-discovery, dedication, and more, like all the best things in life. *The key is to make the "work" enjoyable!*

Transparency

Having spent decades in the pit of internal hell, I've been humbled so severely that I know in the depths of my soul that I am no better or worse than any human being. I've seen and experienced tremendous pain and loss, like many others. But the universe brought darkness into my life to help me appreciate the light. And after reaching my lowest points, I can say, with absolute certainty, the highs are worth it.

But I'm no saint and have never professed to be one. Where should I begin? I dated during the first three of our 6-year separation. That's cheating since I was still married, despite the "technicality." I was a functional alcoholic for many years and spent 48 hours in jail for a DUI during the divorce process. I couldn't hold a job nor manage the money I earned. My poor wife and children have been subjected to my volatile moods far too long, and I've been a horrible friend to so many great people. If I were coaching Gina 10 years ago, I would have told her to leave me too.

For all my failings as a husband and father, I've been on the brink of taking my life more times than I'd like to count. But after being at my worst, I appreciate "the best" more than ever.

Over-Share Alert! No, cancel the alert because I believe in 100% openness and honesty, just like 100% responsibility. I have modeled these principles in this book. Why be so transparent? I'm an open book because it's **not about me**. It's about being a *"force for good"* (based on a Love Supreme) and connecting with people of diverse worldviews, backgrounds, and belief systems. The more I share, the more others can relate and know that they're not alone.

Openness is the best way to find common ground. That being said, by reading this book, you've agreed to a "social contract" of respecting my vulnerability because it's intended only to help others. Therefore, all "negative Nelly's" and trolls, who have nothing beneficial to spew other than venom, you are already under your own judgment; your negativity will be reflected back to you (even with a fake profile). That's why Christ warned us not to judge others because the measure we use for them will be measured to <u>our thoughts and actions</u>. It's timeless wisdom spoken almost 2,000 years before social media, TV, and the Internet. And if you're a Christian with judgment and condemnation in your heart, read Christ's example in <u>John 8: 1-11</u>.

Whenever you disparage another person (to their face or behind their back), it says less about them than it says about you. And when someone places you on a pedestal, don't let it go to your head. That's a reflection of the admirer's capacity to love, appreciate, and admire others. That being said, I am grateful to everyone who takes the time and energy to share their thoughts and reactions to my work. It's all great to hear, especially if you disagree. I only ask that you extend the same kindness, grace, love, and respect you would want if you put your inner-most thoughts in a book for the world to read...

One of my favorite quotes is from the brilliant Dr. Cornel West on a 2019 Joe Rogan Experience (JRE) podcast. He sums-up exactly how I feel about life, purpose, and what inspired this work:

"All we can do, as human beings, is to try and inspire one another, and encourage one another, and enable one another, ennoble one another, and that, in and of itself, is what the great John Coltrane called 'a force for good.' How do I become, based on a Love Supreme, 'a force for good' in a cold and cruel world? ...and Love Supreme is not love in the abstract, right? It's a love of beauty in its concrete forms, it's a love of goodness in its concrete forms, it's a love of truth in its concrete forms..."

"...and [I] know Judaism, Christianity, Islam, all these religions, for me, have no wholesale monopoly on how we understand the world, 'cause they all emerged at various historical moments; but when it comes to this love that allows us to persist in a world [with] cruelty and envy, contempt, manipulation, dishonesty... and that's shot through all of us, so we're not finger-pointing and name-calling... we're talking about the human condition."

-Dr. Cornel West – JRE #1325 – 07/24/19

This book was written, along my journey, as journal entries whenever an insight was received during meditation or a nugget of wisdom helped me through a tough time. I did not intend to write a book; but I wanted to share what I learned to help others. For many years, meditation was my only refuge. When your entire world feels like it's against you (even your own family), you have to reach deep within for the strength to stand in your truth. And I wanted to share what inspired me during my deepest meditations.

I use all the techniques I've shared with you, to this day. To quote the cliché, "I practice what I preach." This is **not** "theory" to me. I believe in this and have seen results with my own eyes.

But this is just the beginning. You have to find your truth, your path. And I hope something in these pages inspires you to achieve your version of Heaven on Earth. Everything is possible when you're aligned with Source!

~~*

With great power comes great responsibility... all 100% of it! And rest assured, I've used the Cleaning Meditation throughout the process of researching, writing, and editing this book. Every page is infused with Divine love and the best intentions to serve the Highest Good of all. However, I am desperately human and quintessentially fallible. If I missed the mark, in any way, please allow me to reconcile with you and God/Source, right now, through the Ho'oponopono:

Please forgive me if I hurt, triggered, offended, or otherwise upset you by anything in this book. I take 100% responsibility for my words, actions, and inactions that caused you pain. And I know, though **un**intended, it still hurts the same.

I pray you're inspired to achieve your heart's desires. As we create Supreme Good, as Love Providers. Thank you for being the powerful, luminous soul thou art. And I love you from the center of my heart.

~b

Just ~b...

A Love Provider!

I Love You Gina!

Bibliography

Primary Sources

BOOKS

Amen, G. Daniel. *Change Your Brain, Change Your Life: The Breakthrough Program for Conquering Anxiety, Depression, Obsessiveness, Lack of Focus, Anger, and Memory Prob.* New York: Harmony Publishing, 2015.

Atwood, Lara. *The Ancient Religion of the Sun: The Wisdom Bringers and The Lost Civilization of the Sun.* Perth: Mystical Life Publications Ltd, 2018.

Bartlett, Richard. *Matrix Energetics: The Science and Art of Transformation.* New York: Astria Books/ Beyond Words Publishing Inc., 2007.

Bilotta, Larry. *Thought War: How To Stop Bad Moods and Feel Like A Million in Minutes.* Thought War Publications Inc., 1993.

Blavatsky, P. Helena. *Isis Unveiled. California*: Theosophical University Press Catalog, 1999.

Braden, Gregg. *Secrets of the Lost Mode of Prayer: The Hidden Power of Beauty, Blessings, Wisdom, And Hurt.* California: Hay House Inc, 2006.

—.*The Divine Matrix: Bridging Time, Space, Miracles, and Belief.* California: Hay House Inc, 2008.

—. *Fractal Time: The Secret of 2012 and a New World Age.* California: Hay House Inc, 2010.

—.*Resilience from the Heart: The Power to Thrive in Life's Extremes.* California: Hay House Inc, 2015.

Chapman, Gary. *The 5 Love Languages: The Secret of Love That Lasts.* Chicago: Moody Publishers, 2015.

Eggerichs, Emerson. *Love and Respect in the Family: The Respect Parents Desire; The Love Children Need.* Colorado Springs: W Publishing Group, 2013.

Gibran, Kahlil. *The Prophet.* New York: The Knopf Doubleday Publishing Group, 1923.

Glover, A. Robert, No More Mr. Nice Guy: A Proven Plan for Getting What You Want in Love, Sex, and Life. Philadelphia: Running Press Adult, 2003.

Gordon, Richard. *Your Healing Hands: The Polarity Experience.* Berkeley: North Atlantic Books, 2004.

Gray, John. *Men Are from Mars, Women Are from Venus.* London: HarperCollins Publishers Inc., 2018.

Hammond, Frank and Ida Mae Hammond. *Pigs in the Parlor: A Practical Guide to Deliverance.* Kirkwood: Impact Christian Books, Inc., 2014.

Harley Jr., Willard F. *His Needs, Her Needs: Building an Affair-Proof Marriage*. Grand Rapids: Fleming H. Revell, 2001.

Hill, Napoleon. *Outwitting the Devil: The Secret to Freedom and Success*. Edited by Sharon L. Lechter. New York: Sterling, 2011.

—.*Think and Grow Rich*. New York: Quarto Group USA Inc., 2015.

Johnson, Spencer. *Who Moved My Cheese? : An Amazing Way to Deal With Change in Your Work and in Your Life*. London: Ebudy Pr., 2002.

Kiyosaki Robert T. and Sharon L. Lechter. *Rich Dad, Poor Dad: What the Rich Teach their Kids About Money- What the Poor and Middle Class Do Not!* New York: Warner Books, 2000.

Laviolette, Darek. *A S.E.A.L. To Heal Your Marriage: A Decorated Navy SEAL's Operational Guide to Heal Your Relationship*. Charleston: Advantage, 2016.

Megre, Vladimir. *The Ringing Cedars*. 8 Vols. Stateline: Ringing Cedars Press, 2008.

Mishlove, Jeffrey and John E. Mack. *The PK Man: A True Story of Mind Over Matter*. Charlottesville: Hampton Roads Publishing Company Inc., 2000.

Peirce, Penney. *Frequency: The Power of Personal Vibration*. New York: Astria Books/ Beyond Words Publishing Inc., 2009.

Robbins, Diane. *Messages from the Hollow Earth*. California: CreateSpace, 2016.

Runkel, Hal Edward and LMFT. *ScreamFree Parenting: The Revolutionary Approach to Raising Your Kids by Keeping Your Cool*. New York: Broadway Books, 2007.

Scheinfeld, Robert. *Busting Loose From the Money Game: Mind-Blowing Strategies for Changing the Rules of a Game You Can't Win*. Hoboken: John Wiley & Sons Inc., 2006.

Talbot, Michael. *The Holographic Universe*. New York: HarperCollins Publishers, 1991.

—. *Mysticism and the New Physics*. London: Penguin Books, 1993.

Tzu, Lao. *Tao Te Ching*. London: Penguin Classics, 2003.

The Emerald Tablets of Thoth The Atlantean. Translated by M. Doreal. Gallatin: Source Books Inc., 2006.

The First and Second Books of Enoch: Translation with Extensive Commentary. Translated by Dr. A. Nyland. Scotts Valley: CreateSpace Independent Publishing Platform, 2011.

Vitale, Joe. *At Zero: The Final Secrets to "Zero Limits" The Quest for Miracles Through Ho'oponopono*. Hoboken: Wiley, 2013.

Vitale, Joe and Ihaleakala Hew Len. *Zero Limits: The Secret Hawaiian System for Wealth, Health, Peace, and More*. Hoboken: Wiley, 2009.

Welsing, Frances Cess. *The Isis Papers: The Keys to the Colors*.

London: C.W. Publishing Group, 2004.

Zeland, Vadim. *Reality Transurfing*. 3 Vols. Ropley: O Books, 2008.

Secondary Sources

ARTICLES

Choi, Q. Charles. "Why Pendulum Clocks Mysteriously Sync Up."

LiveScience, July 23, 2015.

https://www.livescience.com/51644-why-pendulum-

clocks-sync-up.html.

Collins, Sonya. "The Loneliness Epidemic Has Very Real

Consequences." *WebMd*,

https://www.webmd.com/balance/features/loneliness-

epidemic-consequences.

Curry, Andrew. "Gobekli Tepe: The World's First Temple?

Predating Stonehenge by 6,000 years, Turkey's stunning

Gobekli Tepe upends the conventional view of the rise of

civilization." *Smithsonian Magazine*, November, 2018.

https://www.smithsonianmag.com/history/gobekli-tepe-

the-worlds-first-temple-83613665/.

Dovey, Dana. "Human brains are able to predict the future before

the eye can tell it what happened." *Newsweek*, May 12,

2017. https://www.newsweek.com/neuroscience-optical-illusions-brain-science-735274.

Dr. Soph. "6 Ways to Switch Off the Fight-or-Flight Response." *Dr Soph*, June 21, 2018. https://drsoph.com/blog/6-ways-to-switch-off-the-fight-or-flight-response.

Fischetti, Mark. "All 2.3 Million Species Are Mapped into a Single Circle of Life: ineages of all known species on earth are finally pieced together." *Scientific American*, December 1, 2016. https://www.scientificamerican.com/article/all-2-3-million-species-are-mapped-into-a-single-circle-of-life/.

Fitzgerald, MacLean. "It's The Simple Stuff That Makes You—And Your Brain—Happy." *Brain Connection*, May 31, 2016. https://brainconnection.brainhq.com/2016/05/31/simple-stuff-makes-brain-happy/.

Fuller, John. "How Warp Speed Works." *Science: How stuff works*, https://science.howstuffworks.com/warp-speed2.htm, https://science.howstuffworks.com/warp-speed3.htm.

Gordon, Donald A. and Jack Arbuthnot. "The Impact of Divorce on Young Children and Adolescents." Divorce Magazine, June 07, 2019. https://www.divorcemag.com/articles/effects-of-divorce-on-children.

Gorman, Christine. "Explore the Human Microbiome [Interactive]: Learn about the bacteria, fungi and other micro-organisms that maintain human health." Scientific American, May 15, 2012.

https://www.scientificamerican.com/article/microbiome-graphic-explore-human-microbiome/.

Hartman, Mitchell. "Here's how much money there is in the world — and why you've never heard the exact number." Business Insider, November 17, 2017.

https://www.businessinsider.com/heres-how-much-money-there-is-in-the-world-2017-10.

Houston, Natalie. "Got a Minute? Count Backwards." The Chronicle of Higher Education, October 29, 2009.

https://www.chronicle.com/blogs/profhacker/got-a-minute-count-backwards/22801.

"How Many Eggs Are Women Born With? And Other Common Questions About Egg Supply."Healthline Parenthood,

https://www.healthline.com/health/womens-health/how-many-eggs-does-a-woman-have#eggs-at-40.

James, Matt. "The Hawaiian Secret of Forgiveness." Psychology Today, May 23, 2011.

https://www.psychologytoday.com/us/blog/focus-forgiveness/201105/the-hawaiian-secret-forgiveness?amp.

Keim, Brandon. "Brain Scanners Can See Your Decisions Before You Make Them." *Wired*, March 13, 2008. https://www.wired.com/2008/04/mind-decision/.

Levy, Jillian. "The Human Microbiome: How It Works + a Diet for Gut Health." *Dr. Axe*, January 7, 2016. https://draxe.com/health/microbiome/.

Lewis, Jordan Gaines. "When It Comes to Color, Men & Women Aren't Seeing Eye to Eye: How does the brain's wiring affect men and women's perception of color?" *Psychology Today*, April 08, 2015. https://www.psychologytoday.com/us/blog/brain-babble/201504/when-it-comes-color-men-women-arent-seeing-eye-eye.

Lodge, Michelle. "Female breadwinners: What it means when mom is the provider." *Fortune,* November 3, 2014. https://fortune.com/2014/11/03/female-breadwinners/.

Martin, F. William. "The Origin of Mitochondria." Scitable: by Nature Education, 2010. https://www.nature.com/scitable/topicpage/the-origin-of-mitochondria-14232356/.

Mosher, Dave. "'Almost everyone' in a photo of Southwest's emergency landing wore their oxygen mask 'wrong,' says a former flight attendant." Business Insider, April 18, 2018.

https://www.businessinsider.com/southwest-emergency-landing-oxygen-masks-incorrectly-worn-1380-2018-4.

Moskowitz, Clara. "Are We Living in a Computer Simulation?" Scientific American, April 7, 2016. https://www.scientificamerican.com/article/are-we-living-in-a-computer-simulation/.

Olson, R. Eric. "Why Are 250 Million Sperm Cells Released During Sex?" Live Science, January 24, 2013. https://www.livescience.com/32437-why-are-250-million-sperm-cells-released-during-sex.html.

Parker, Kim and Renee Stepler. "Americans see men as the financial providers, even as women's contributions grow." Pew Research Center, September 20, 2017. https://www.pewresearch.org/fact-tank/2017/09/20/americans-see-men-as-the-financial-providers-even-as-womens-contributions-grow/.

Perry, Philip." The mystery of how birds navigate is over, and the answer is so amazing." Big Think, April 12, 2018. https://bigthink.com/philip-perry/the-mystery-of-how-birds-navigate-is-over-and-the-answer-is-so-amazing.

Pickhardt, E. Carl. "The Impact of Divorce on Young Children and Adolescents." Psychology Today, December 19, 2011. https://www.psychologytoday.com/us/blog/surviving-your-childs-adolescence/201112/the-impact-divorce-young-children-and-adolescents.

Pilkington, Mark. "Zero Point Energy." The Guardian, July 17, 2003. https://www.theguardian.com/education/2003/jul/17/research.highereducation.

Rana, Tania. "The 12 Best Ancient Temples in India You Should Visit." Culture Trip, FEBRUARY 20, 2018. https://theculturetrip.com/asia/india/articles/ancient-temples-india-you-should-visit/.

Schirber, Michael. "The Chemistry of Life: The Human Body." Live Science, April 16, 2009. https://www.livescience.com/3505-chemistry-life-human-body.html.

Segal, Jeanne, Melinda Smith and Greg Boose. "Nonverbal Communication." Help Guide, June 2019. https://www.helpguide.org/articles/relationships-communication/nonverbal-communication.htm.

Spector, Dina. "Here's how many days a person can survive without water." Business Insider,   March 8, 2018. https://www.businessinsider.com/how-many-days-can-you-survive-without-water-2014-5.

Sundermier, Ali. "The particle physics of you." Symmetry, 11 March, 2015. https://www.symmetrymagazine.org/article/the-particle-physics-of-you.

Tarantola, Andrew. "Why Frame Rate Matters." Gizmodo, January 14, 15. https://gizmodo.com/why-frame-rate-matters-1675153198.

Tommasini, Anthony. "The Art of Setting the Senses on Edge." The New York Times, May 30, 2014. https://www.nytimes.com/2014/06/01/arts/music/musical-dissonance-from-schumann-to-sondheim.html.

Trafton, Anne. "In the blink of an eye: MIT neuroscientists find the brain can identify images seen for as little as 13 milliseconds." MIT News Office, January 16, 2014. http://news.mit.edu/2014/in-the-blink-of-an-eye-0116.

Vitale, Joe. "Simple Steps to Healing: Ho'oponopono: I Love You, I'm Sorry, Please Forgive Me, Thank You." *Want to Know*, https://www.wanttoknow.info/070701imsorryiloveyoujoevitale.

Wong, Kate. "Tiny Genetic Differences between Humans and Other Primates Pervade the Genome." *Scientific American*, September 1, 2014. https://www.scientificamerican.com/article/tiny-genetic-differences-between-humans-and-other-primates-

pervade-the-genome/.

Yancey-Bragg, N'dea. "The black hole at the center of our galaxy

just lit up twice as bright as ever. Who knows why." *USA

Today*, August 14, 2019.

https://eu.usatoday.com/story/news/nation/2019/08/13/

black-hole-center-our-galaxy-lit-up-puzzling-

astronomers/2003939001/.

"Your Reality Is an Illusion." *HuffPost*, July 22, 2011.

https://www.huffpost.com/entry/reality-

illusion_b_847079.

CLASSES

Brain Fit Life. Amen, Daniel. Online Class, 2017.

Hypnosis Session. Oxley, Morgan. Portland: Session, January 24th,

2012.

Love & Respect Conference and 10 Week Study. Eggerichs,

Emerson and Sarah Eggerichs. McKinney: Conference,

2017. Completed, 2019.

Scientific Thinking and Communication. Tyson, Neil DeGrasse:

MasterClass. Completed, 2019.

Self-Identity Through Ho'oponopono IZI, LLC. Oregon: Class, 2014.

Self-Identity Through Ho'oponopono. Hawaii (via Absentee): Class, 2014.

Silva Ultramind Course. Jose Silva. Course, 2007.

Speed Reading. Giuliano, Jackie Alan. Seattle: Workshop, 2013.

The Environment Changer Course. Bilotta, Larry. Oconomowoc: Course, 2012.

DICTIONARIES

Know Your Phrase, s.v. "Everything but The Kitchen Sink,"
https://knowyourphrase.com/everything-but-the-kitchen-sink.

Merriam-Webster, s.v. "harmony,"
https://www.merriam-webster.com/dictionary/harmony.

ENCYCLOPEDIAS

Encyclopedia Britannica. s.v "Physiology." Chicago: Encyclopedia Britannica, 2019.
https://www.britannica.com/science/information-theory/Physioloy.

JOURNALS

Gardner, Benjamin, Phillippa Lally and Jane Wardle. "Making health habitual: the psychology of 'habit-formation' and general practice." *NCBI*, (2012): 664–666. doi: 10.3399/bjgp12X659466.

Gilbert, A. Jack and Josh D. Neufeld. "Life in a World without Microbes." *NCBI*, (2014)   doi: 10.1371/journal.pbio.1002020.

Nordmann, C. Gregory, Tobias Hochstoeger and David A. Keays. "Magnetoreception—A sense without a receptor." *Plos: Biology*, no. 2 (2017). doi:/10.1371/*journal.pbio.2003234.*

SC, Gandevia, Wilson LR, Inglis JT, and Burke D. "Mental rehearsal of motor tasks recruits alpha-motoneurones but fails to recruit human fusimotorneurones selectively." NCBI, no.1 (1997): 259-66. doi: 10.1111/j.1469-7793.1997.259bc.x.

MOVIES

Inside Out. Directed by Pete Docter and Ronnie Del Carmen. 2015. Emeryville, CA: Pixar Animation Studios and Walt Disney Pictures, 2015, DVD.

The Matrix. Directed by Lana Wachowski and Lilly Wachowski. 1999. Sydney, AU: Warner Bros, 1999, DVD.

VIDEOS

1RiotKing. "The Matrix Reloaded - The Architect Scene 1080p Part 1." YouTube video, 4:46. March 1, 2017.

https://www.youtube.com/watch?v=cHZl2naX1Xk&feature=youtu.be.

AiirSource Military. "Marine Corps Scout Sniper Course: Cover and Concealment." YouTube video, 7:19 November 22, 2017. https://www.youtube.com/watch?v=44-i3SSzXCY&feature=youtu.be.

Ancient Architects. "Acoustic Levitation in Egypt - Ancient High Technology | Ancient Architects." YouTube video, 12:30. January 3, 2018. https://www.youtube.com/watch?v=rcFWn3-i8F0.

Ancient Explorers. "Heart Mind Coherence." YouTube video, 8:30. May 24, 2016. https://www.youtube.com/watch?v=iYRtFt2UTOA&feature=youtu.be.

Andrew Kirby. "Society's Biggest Lie." YouTube video, 9:34. April 5, 2019, https://www.youtube.com/watch?v=OytlMHkUKdM&feature=youtu.be.

Andy Dufresne. "Matrix Revolutions- Final Battle Scene." YouTube video, 5:33. May 8, 2014. https://www.youtube.com/watch?v=lX0Do0-5vKs&feature=youtu.be.

Aperture. "How Short Your Life REALLY Is." YouTube video, 10:32.
December 5, 2018.
https://www.youtube.com/watch?v=qkEq-
YVn8Ew&feature=youtu.be.

AsapSCIENCE. "The Periodic Table Song." YouTube video, 2:53.
October 31, 2015.
https://www.youtube.com/watch?v=VgVQKCcfwnU&featu
re=youtu.be.

Be Inspired. "A Must See!!! The Most Eye Opening 10 Minutes of
Your Life | Dr. Bruce Lipton (PART 2)" YouTube video,
10:10. May 7, 2019.
https://www.youtube.com/watch?v=jDVi7pCEzu8&featur
e=youtu.be.

Be Inspired. "Mantak Chia: Techniques to Activate the Second
Brain." YouTube video, 14:10. December 5, 2018,
https://www.youtube.com/watch?v=kaefdiE4ovk&feature
=youtu.be.

Be Inspired. "The No.1 Habit Billionaires Run Daily." YouTube
video, 10:02. February 12, 2019.
https://www.youtube.com/watch?v=2iPFtZENEq4&featur
e=youtu.be.

Beyond Science. "Is Water ALIVE?! Water Responds to Our Words,
Music & Even Thoughts." YouTube video, 4:34. November

14, 2015.

https://www.youtube.com/watch?v=IYRPy2G4TKs&featur
e=youtu.be.

Big Think. "Is time real or is it an illusion? | Michelle Thaller."
YouTube video, 5:11. March 12,
2019.https://www.youtube.com/watch?v=86RI1G1J2p8.

Big Think. "Become an intellectual explorer: Master the art of
conversation | Emily Chamlee-Wright." YouTube video,
5:24. July 17, 2019,
https://www.youtube.com/watch?v=AWUDFge4t-
4&feature=youtu.be.

Braden, Gregg. "Ensuring Humanity's Continuation." Gaia video,
31:00. March 23, 2017.
https://www.gaia.com/video/ensuring-humanitys-
continuation.

Breaking Convention. "Rupert Sheldrake - Psychedelic Experience
And Morphic Resonance." YouTube video, 25:36. July 10,
2017.
https://www.youtube.com/watch?v=8cAYO0Bwpa4&featu
re=emb_logo.

British Heart Foundation. "When do our hearts first start to
beat?" YouTube video, 1:32. October 12, 2016.
https://www.youtube.com/watch?v=w9IwUpsBpe0.

Certifiably Ingame. "Fluidic Space: What is it?" YouTube video,
14:33. May 26, 2019,
https://www.youtube.com/watch?v=BoO0x2q2Zuw&featu
re=youtu.be.

Chad Sexington. "Sound Vibration Creates Form (David Icke)."
YouTube video, 4:33. March 2, 2012,
https://www.youtube.com/watch?v=3G5sV6DXQd0&featu
re=youtu.be.

Charisma on Command. "Attachment Theory - How Your
Childhood Affects Your Love Style". YouTube Video, 18:08.
May 15, 2017.
https://www.youtube.com/watch?v=RSlc9IxdBw8&featur
e=youtu.be.

Christopher Bross. "MRI Heartbeat." YouTube video, 0:53.
February 9, 2013.
https://www.youtube.com/watch?v=4B_rHf-
J95U&autoplay=1&app=desktop.

Dana Claudat. "Dr. Emoto's Awesome Rice Experiment + Your
Super powerful Intention!" YouTube video, 5:58.
November 1, 2017.
https://www.youtube.com/watch?v=uDPH18o4dbE&featu
re=youtu.be.

Dry Bar Comedy. "Understanding The Wife's Code. Jeff Allen." YouTube video, 5:06. February 26, 2019. https://www.youtube.com/watch?v=ccTYpVUP4kA&feature=youtu.be.

Ed Plas. "Matrix Déjà vu." YouTube video, 3:59. December 10, 2013. https://www.youtube.com/watch?v=akvRTybPbBE&feature=youtu.be.

F1LT3R. "You're Faster than This." YouTube video, 0:34. February 7, 2014. https://www.youtube.com/watch?v=NqxSgp385N0&feature=youtu.be.

Freestyler 365. "The Matrix (1999) - The Pill scene." YouTube video, 4:41. May 18, 2011. https://www.youtube.com/watch?v=zQ1_IbFFbzA&feature=youtu.be.

Fuzzy Logic. "The Flash - Phasing Speedforce." YouTube video, 2:04. April 1, 2015. https://www.youtube.com/watch?v=GW4oDf80GRY&feature=youtu.be.

GreatCall. "What is the Difference Between Cellular and Wi-Fi Data?" YouTube video, 1:58. May 21, 2015. https://www.youtube.com/watch?v=-bSiNVUCLG0.

Growth Events. "How to Manifesting Prayer Work - Gregg
Braden." YouTube video, 8:O6. July 11, 2018
https://www.youtube.com/watch?v=q34NNVFUc7I.

Gundersen Health System. "HeartMath Quick Coherence
Technique." YouTube video, 3:55.October 22, 2012.
https://www.youtube.com/watch?v=8zHuoU8yKLQ&featu
re=youtu.be.

Halo Media Works. "Medical Animation | Heart." YouTube video,
0:20. August 5, 2015.
https://www.youtube.com/watch?v=q0gOkOlcYU0.

Hamnoj. "Monty Python and the Holy Grail - The Insulting
Frenchman." YouTube video, 2:09. July 30, 2008.
https://www.youtube.com/watch?v=QSo0duY7-
9s&feature=youtu.be.

Harleen Quinzel. "Star Wars: The Clone Wars - Yoda vs. Dark Yoda
[1080p]." YouTube video, 3:25. July 10, 2015.
https://www.youtube.com/watch?v=ctoWE_2iJOw&featur
e=youtu.be.

HarvardX. "Mitochondria: the cell's powerhouse." YouTube video,
5:16. April 19, 2017.
https://www.youtube.com/watch?v=vkYEYjintqU&feature
=youtu.be.

HeartMath Institute. "The Heart's Intuitive Intelligence: A path to personal, social and global coherence." YouTube video, 7:19. April 22, 2013. https://www.youtube.com/watch?v=QdneZ4fIIHE.

HeartMath Institute. "Science of the Heart." YouTube video, 1:36. April 16, 2010. https://www.youtube.com/watch?v=pp-r_f8-qz8&feature=youtu.be.

Hinkmond. "Q-36 Space Modulator." YouTube video, 0:37. July 16, 2011. https://www.youtube.com/watch?v=QuUJfYcn3V4.

Ho'oponopono Seminars. "Ho'oponopono Dr Hew Len 100% Responsibility." YouTube video, 4:27. April 26, 2016. https://www.youtube.com/watch?v=-qqH6SGGNtg&feature=youtu.be.

Ho'oponopono Seminars. "Ho'oponopono Mantra to Whom." YouTube video, 2:58. April 26. 2016, https://www.youtube.com/watch?v=V_Q3I4IaV9s&feature=youtu.be.

It's Just Astronomical! "The Earth Is Wobbling: The Precession of the Equinoxes." YouTube video, 5:49. April 7, 2017. https://www.youtube.com/watch?v=adzx547ptck.

Jason Headley. "It's Not About The Nail." YouTube video, 1:41. May 22, 2013. https://www.youtube.com/watch?v=-4EDhdAHrOg&feature=youtu.be.

Jemyao. "A Tale of Two Brains - Men's Brain Women's Brain - Mark Gungor." YouTube video, 13:34. October 31, 2012. https://www.youtube.com/watch?v=29JPnJSmDs0.

John Izzo. "5 Words That Will Improve Your Ability to Receive Feedback." YouTube video, 5:14. April 1, 2014. https://www.youtube.com/watch?v=4BpPtjKpJZM&feature=youtu.be-.

Jonathan Jacks. "The Physics of Roadrunner - Balloon Anvil." YouTube video, 1:08. August 19, 2015. https://www.youtube.com/watch?v=e7K1Sgywkil&feature=youtu.be.

Jordan Peterson Fan Channel. "The Real Reason for Marriage - Prof. Jordan Peterson." YouTube video, 5:53. July 21, 2017. https://www.youtube.com/watch?v=Rc_NNjVOs1o&feature=youtu.be.

Jomomomo. "That Bitch Crazy." YouTube video, 3:48. March 9, 2007. https://www.youtube.com/watch?v=FxevxvvAKrM&feature=youtu.be.

Kaspersky. "What is a Firewall?" YouTube video, 1:53. January 25, 2018,. https://www.youtube.com/watch?v=x1YLj06c3hM.

KClassScienceChannel. "Size of light source and sharpness of shadow | Light | Physics." YouTube video 0:56. July 5, 2013. https://www.youtube.com/watch?v=rkm3souCAg8.

Kurzgesagt – In a Nutshell. "How Bacteria Rule Over Your Body – The Microbiome." YouTube video, 7:38. October 5, 2017. https://www.youtube.com/watch?v=VzPDO09qTN4&feature=youtu.be.

Laina. "Sock Puppet Show." YouTube video, 3:14. January 21, 2016. https://www.youtube.com/watch?v=w-_0WYjtxrE.

Lincoln Bain. "The most powerful secret on earth! So powerful both Jesus and Satan used it!" YouTube video, 8:38. July 30, 2017. https://www.youtube.com/watch?v=x8DqhWYwSCQ&feature=youtu.be.

London Real. "How nature and balance work - Gregg Braden | London Real." YouTube video, 2:22. March 12, 2018. https://www.youtube.com/watch?v=ENVZn7AfClk.

London Real. "The Fundamental Rule of Nature is Cooperation- Gregg Braden | London Real." YouTube video, 5:11. November 25, 2018. https://www.youtube.com/watch?v=v_EpDbjDm70

Looper. "The Untold Truth Of They Live." YouTube video, 5:22. September 22, 2018.

https://www.youtube.com/watch?v=BSnWDrKJVXU&featu
re=youtu.be.

Mantak Chia. "Mantak Chia Inner Smile for daily life practice."
YouTube video, 10:10. January 26, 2009.
https://www.youtube.com/watch?v=P7jXd6Qt1DM&featu
re=youtu.be.

Marcelo Zuniga. "Darth Vader's Death - Return of the Jedi (1983
Eyebrows)." YouTube video, 2:24. February 3, 2015.
https://www.youtube.com/watch?v=TNDwCsFzS8c&featu
re=youtu.be.

Mayo Clinic. "Seeing Inside the Heart With MRI - Mayo Clinic,"
YouTube video, 1:46. February 22, 2011
https://www.youtube.com/watch?v=IGyeNtZZnrk.

mccainisthroughX. "We Are All Black - Geneticist Bryan Sykes."
YouTube video, 8:26. April 27, 2012.
https://www.youtube.com/watch?v=2jTAueCy4O0&t=29s.

Mel Robbins. "Mel Robbins: How to have difficult conversations."
YouTube video, 4:49. October 19, 2018.
https://www.youtube.com/watch?v=TQ48GVMfvMg.

Mementh. "Axe Bow Chica Wow Wow 2." YouTube video, 0:30.
May 25, 2007.
https://www.youtube.com/watch?v=9BmV9aWqm2E&fea
ture=youtu.be.

Military Life. "Recon Marines – 'This is Recon's Life' || Military Motivation 2019." YouTube video, 4:14 November 2, 2019. https://www.youtube.com/watch?v=uZeUMbDd7i8&feature=youtu.be.

Morning Star. "TRON- Legacy - Kevin Flynn and Clu (Final Confrontation)_HD.mp4." YouTube video, 4:44. December 31, 2016. https://www.youtube.com/watch?v=mLxnnDemvL4&feature=youtu.be.

Movieclips Classic Trailers. "Groundhog Day (1993) Trailer #1 | Movieclips Classic Trailers." YouTube video, 2:39. February 2, 2018. https://www.youtube.com/watch?v=GncQtURdcE4&feature=youtu.be.

mushin111. "Cardiac MRI scan of a heart beating in high resolution – ECG gated CMRI in HD - real time scan." YouTube video, 3:14. February 11, 2011. https://www.youtube.com/watch?v=G4dFVeP9Vdo.

Nate Woodbury. "How To Improve Communication With Your Spouse." YouTube video, 14:02. June 9, 2017. https://www.youtube.com/watch?v=c5AJbOd794U&feature=youtu.be.

n e1. "Morphic Resonance and Consciousness Mind Tuning."
YouTube video, 36:16. September 9, 2015.
https://www.youtube.com/watch?v=tj6k0If90tQ&feature
=youtu.be.

Nigel John Stanford. "CYMATICS: Science Vs. Music - Nigel
Stanford." YouTube video, 5:52. November 12, 2014.
https://www.youtube.com/watch?v=Q3oItpVa9fs.

Noise Fear Buddies. "Dr. Karen L. Overall: Techniques For
Encouraging Dogs to Relax." YouTube video, 13:05.
January 5, 2019.
https://www.youtube.com/watch?v=bdffTkxqlZQ.

Now This World, "These Are The World's Oldest Countries."
YouTube video, 3:44. January 22, 2017.
https://www.youtube.com/watch?v=4jmXArRmmmk&feat
ure=youtu.be.

Peter Breggin MD. "How to Help the Suicidally Depressed Person--
Dr. Peter Breggin's 5th 'Simple Truths About Psychiatry'."
YouTube video, 10:24. September 20, 2013.
https://www.youtube.com/watch?v=t7OPWRqjaSQ&featu
re=youtu.be.

PowerfulJRE. "Joe Rogan Experience #1325 - Dr. Cornel West."
YouTube video, 1:58:20. July 24, 2019.
https://www.youtube.com/watch?v=ViWvAnvT17c.

Practical Psychology. "How to Never Run out of Things to Say - Keep a Conversation Flowing!." YouTube video, 7:39. December 13, 2016.https://www.youtube.com/watch?v=vU-ibdHkz4Y&feature=youtu.be.

Practical Psychology. "MicroExpressions - Reading Facial Expressions Are Better than Reading Body Language." YouTube video, 7:46. December 2, 2017. https://www.youtube.com/watch?v=tu1uzG_EBGM.

Sarastarlight. "Limbic System: Sex, Hallucinations, Emotion, Memory, PTSD, Amygdala... Brain Mind Lecture 6." YouTube video, 53:30. December 9, 2006. https://www.youtube.com/watch?v=T7nXiXQb2iM&feature=youtu.be.

Scarakus. "Hans Jenny's - Cymatic Soundscapes." YouTube video, 28:03. October 10, 2014. https://www.youtube.com/watch?v=D2JeHlFtMDM&feature=youtu.be.

SCC Digital Video Productions. "The Narrative Film: The Illusion of Movement." YouTube video, 5:26. June 3, 2010. https://www.youtube.com/watch?v=CBHOny0R7_o.

Science Channel. "Do Transplanted Organs Carry Memories?"
YouTube video, 2:26. October 23, 2014.
https://www.youtube.com/watch?v=GXKxIGn0YZo.

SciShow. "The Next Step to a Holodeck." YouTube video, 4:47.
October 29, 2017.
https://www.youtube.com/watch?v=9U3RYNwsUHM&fea
ture=youtu.be.

SciShow Psych. "Are There "Male" and "Female" Brains?"
YouTube video, 6:55. June 18, 2018.
https://www.youtube.com/watch?v=z5c7ubF0u-
U&feature=youtu.be.

Seeker. "There Are Tiny Mites Living On Your Face!" YouTube
video, 2:38. September 3, 2014.
https://www.youtube.com/watch?v=rJPpdoUsheY&featur
e=youtu.be.

Simple Truths. "The 100 0 Principle." YouTube video, 2:33.
January 27, 2011.
https://www.youtube.com/watch?v=HdJkk_fOJPY&featur
e=youtu.be.

Star Trek Clips. "Data on the Holodeck | Star Trek: The Next
Generation - Encounter at Farpoint." YouTube video, 3:26.
June 10, 2017.

https://www.youtube.com/watch?v=kzNVkc4gB6U&feature=youtu.be.

Star Wars Theory. "The Grey Jedi & Everything You Need to Know – Star Wars Explained." YouTube video, 4:31. September 10, 2016. https://www.youtube.com/watch?v=vfY7lpXAVFQ.

StoneAgeMan. "Symbiosis: Mutualism, Commensalism, and Parasitism." YouTube video, 5:16. January 15, 2012. https://www.youtube.com/watch?v=zSmL2F1t81Q.

Success Archive. "One Of The Most Enlightened Scientists Alive - Nassim Haramein." YouTube video, 10:35. November 19, 2019. https://www.youtube.com/watch?v=GbZO1ykipj0.

Tanglebrook. "Transformers / Transforming Deluxe [1080p]." YouTube video, 10:04. February 2. 2014, https://www.youtube.com/watch?v=rtu62Gklgso&feature=youtu.be.

TED. "How to practice emotional first aid | Guy Winch." YouTube video, 17:28. February 16, 2015. https://www.youtube.com/watch?v=F2hc2FLOdhI&feature=youtu.be.

TED. "You aren't at the mercy of your emotions -- your brain creates them | Lisa Feldman Barrett." YouTube video,

18:28. January 23, 2018.

https://www.youtube.com/watch?v=0gks6ceq4eQ.

TEDx Talks. "Body language, the power is in the palm of your

hands | Allan Pease | TEDxMacquarieUniversity." YouTube

video, 14:29. November 17, 2013.

https://www.youtube.com/watch?v=ZZZ7k8cMA-4.

TEDx Talks. "Communication is ruining your relationships | Beth

Luwandi Lofstrom | TEDxGustavusAdolphusCollege."

YouTube video, 14:43. April 5, 2017.

https://www.youtube.com/watch?v=IT1o2esE_88&featur

e=youtu.be.

TEDx Talks. "Marriage 2.0 -- a system update for lifelong

relationships | Liza Shaw | TEDxHickory." YouTube video,

18:22. July 14, 2014.

https://www.youtube.com/watch?v=IAC8IEJDxCg&feature

=youtu.be.

TEDx Talks. "TEDxDanubia 2011 | Julian Treasure | Conscious

Listening." YouTube video, 19:30. April 16, 2011.

https://www.youtube.com/watch?v=CKayQthlwts.

TEDx Talks. "The Fourth Phase of Water: Dr. Gerald Pollack at

TEDxGuelphU." YouTube video, 24:14. September 6, 2013.

https://www.youtube.com/watch?v=i-

T7tCMUDXU&feature=youtu.be.

TEDx Talks. "The Secret to Understanding Humans | Larry C.

Rosen | TEDxsalinas." YouTube video, 18:08. May 15,

2017.

https://www.youtube.com/watch?v=RSlc9IxdBw8&featur

e=youtu.be.

The G2C. "Morpheus explains what is real." YouTube video, 1:48.

March 26, 2017. https://www.youtube.com/watch?v=t-

Nz6us7DUA&feature=youtu.be.

TronixTheCat. Human beings are a disease, a cancer of this

planet." YouTube video, 1:18. August 2, 2009.

https://www.youtube.com/watch?v=IM1-DQ2Wo_w.

Veritasium. "Empty Space is NOT Empty." YouTube video, 4:45.

April 30, 2013.

https://www.youtube.com/watch?v=J3xLuZNKhlY.

Video Advice. "DANDAPANI: "This was Kept Secret by Monks" | It

Takes Only 4 Days." YouTube video, 10:01. May 9, 2019.

https://www.youtube.com/watch?v=KpD0AdcnbRI&featur

e=youtu.be.

Video Advice. ""Every Billionaire Uses It!"." YouTube video, 10:01.

May 22, 2019.

https://www.youtube.com/watch?v=joQPAk9-

WOE&feature=youtu.be.

Vox. "You have more than five senses." YouTube video, 4:23.

September 19, 2017.

https://www.youtube.com/watch?v=9W0WPPpCFaM.

Weedran. "The Matrix - Battery," YouTube video, 1:32. November

9, 2008.

https://www.youtube.com/watch?v=IojqOMWTgv8&featu

re=youtu.be.

What If. "What If Time Is an Illusion?" YouTube video, 4:40.

February 25, 2019.

https://www.youtube.com/watch?v=ME3jezuckE.

Wise Wanderer. "Great Animation Shows How Deep Humans Dug

into The Earth." YouTube video, 2:53. October 17, 2017.

https://www.youtube.com/watch?v=t6rpafKHbc4.

Wisdom 2.0. "A 15 Minute Mind-Hack to Massively Enhance Your

Brain Power and Emotional State: Vishen Lakhiani."

YouTube video, 35:48. January 20, 2015.

https://www.youtube.com/watch?v=waYNEDZxEPY&featu

re=youtu.be.

Your Youniverse. "How to Align With The Energy of Money &

Abundance - Powerful Law of Attraction Technique!"

YouTube video, 10:22. November 26, 2017.

https://www.youtube.com/watch?v=xXPYjE8o-

rI&feature=youtu.be.

WEBSITES

American Foundation for Suicide Prevention. "Children, Teens and
Suicide Loss." https://afsp.org/find-support/ive-lost-
someone/resources-loss-survivors/children-teens-suicide-
loss/.

American Foundation for Suicide Prevention. "Suicide Statistics."
Last modified 2017. https://afsp.org/about-
suicide/suicide-statistics/.

American Museum of Natural History. "Building Your Microbiome
from Birth." https://www.amnh.org/exhibitions/the-
secret-world-inside-you/microbiome-at-birth.

Association for Safe International Road Travel. "Road safety
facts." https://www.asirt.org/safe-travel/road-safety-
facts/.

Decoding Science Staff. "What is 'Group Think'? Mob Rule and
Society."
https://www.decodedscience.org/what-is-group-think-
mob-rule-and-society/.

Googolplex.com. http://www.googolplex.com/.

Harvard Health Publishing. "Understanding the stress response:
Chronic activation of this survival mechanism impairs
health." Updated: May 1, 2018.

https://www.health.harvard.edu/staying-healthy/understanding-the-stress-response.

Health Resources & Services Administration. "The "Loneliness Epidemic"." Last Reviewed: January 17, 2019.

HeartMath. https://www.heartmath.com/.

Investopedia. "Money." Staff Author. Updated November 7, 2019. https://www.investopedia.com/terms/m/money.asp.

IZI LLC. "Who's In Charge?" https://www.self-i-dentity-through-hooponopono.com/whos-in-charge/.

James Clear. "How Long Does it Actually Take to Form a New Habit? (Backed by Science)." https://jamesclear.com/new-habit.

James L. McGaugh. "Panel: The Science of Memory and Emotion "How Emotions Strengthen Memory"." The Decade of the Brain. http://www.loc.gov/loc/brain/emotion/Mcgaugh.html.

Marriage Missions. https://marriagemissions.com/.

National Institute of General Medical Sciences. "Circadian Rhythms." Revised August 2017. https://www.nigms.nih.gov/education/pages/factsheet_circadianrhythms.aspx.

Navy Seal Foundation. "About the Navy Seals: The Quiet Warriors Who Protect Our Country."

https://www.navysealfoundation.org/who-we-serve/about-the-seals/.

ProFlowers. "51 Types of Flowers Common in the U.S." ProFlowers (blog), Last Updated: March 18, 2019. https://www.proflowers.com/blog/types-of-flowers.

Psych-K. https://psych-k.com/. https://www.hrsa.gov/enews/past-issues/2019/january-17/loneliness-epidemic.

Radiation Answers. "Ionizing Radiation." Radiation Answers. https://www.radiationanswers.org/radiation-introduction/types-of-radiation/ionizing-radiation.html.

Radiation Answers. "Nonionizing Radiation." Radiation Answers. https://www.radiationanswers.org/radiation-introduction/types-of-radiation/non-ionizing-radiation.html.

Robbins, Mel. "The five elements of of the 5 second rule." Mel Robbins (blog), published April 25, 2018. https://melrobbins.com/blog/five-elements-5-second-rule/.

Schmidt Ocean Institute. "The Ocean: Haven't we already mapped it?" https://schmidtocean.org/cruise-log-post/the-ocean-havent-we-already-mapped-it/.

Smithsonian Magazine. "A Decades-Long Quest to Drill Into Earth's Mantle May Soon Hit Pay Dirt." https://www.smithsonianmag.com/science-nature/decades-long-quest-drill-earths-mantle-may-soon-hit-pay-dirt-180957908/.

Spd Rdng. "Conscious vs subconscious processing power." Speed Reader (blog), published August 26, 2009. http://spdrdng.com/posts/conscious-vs-subconscious-processing.

The Matrix 101. "The Matrix Revolutions: Meaning & Interpretations." Last modified 2014. http://thematrix101.com/revolutions/meaning.php.

The Matrix-Wiki. "Deus Ex Machina." https://matrix.fandom.com/wiki/Deus_Ex_Machina.

Ubuntu Contributionism. https://www.ubuntucontributionism.org/.

University of Copenhagen: The Faculty of Health and Medical Sciences. "Molecular mechanisms behind women's biological clock." ScienceDaily. www.sciencedaily.com/releases/2019/10/191009101143.htm.

Vanderblit University. "Homework Answer Key: Homework 1."

https://www.vanderbilt.edu/AnS/physics/astrocourses/AS

T101/homework/hw1key.html.

Vangie Beal. "CPU - Central Processing Unit." Webopedia.

https://www.webopedia.com/TERM/C/CPU.html.

Wordometer. "Real time world statistics." Wordometers.

https://www.worldometers.info/.

Ho'oponopono

For more information on the SITH Ho'oponopono Classes, please go to the OFFICIAL website: https://www.self-i-dentity-through-hooponopono.com/

Note: There are some fraudulent and plagiarized sites out there. Please ensure that the website is the official class endorsed by Dr. Ihaleakala Hew Len (listed above).

Environment Changers

For more information on the EC (Environment Changer) program, please go to the following websites:

For Men: http://itonlytakesoneman.com/ and https://youcansavethismarriage.com/ec-for-men/

For Women: http://itonlytakesonewoman.com/

Flag Page: https://www.flagpage.com/

Index

Additional Help For Suicide Prevention
(Please add these to your 'Contacts')

SAMHSA National Helpline
1-800-662-HELP (4357)
www.samhsa.gov/find-help/national-helpline

Teen2Teen Helpline
1-877-968-8491
Or Text "Teen2Teen" to 839863

National Suicide Prevention Lifeline
1-800-273-TALK (8255)
TTY: 1-800-799-4889
www.suicidepreventionlifeline.org

Counseling Resources:
www.psychology.com
www.betterhelp.com
www.talkspace.com
https://cimhs.com/

Life and death is one choice away. Choose life and live to love another day!

In Their Words

Taking a spiritual approach, men are instilled with an unshakable sense of hope and purpose.
–Eva Xan
Author/Artist - USA

The author came across as trustworthy, authentic, and healed! I felt particular empathy over struggles with mental health which for men - especially black men - are overlooked far too often.
–Stephanie Francis
Life Coach/Educator - UK

As a step-by-step guide on how to achieve personal enlightenment and empowerment, Patridge's book offers men life-changing solutions to life's tumultuous issues.
–David Connolly
Author/Editor/Publishing Consultant – USA

I'm so excited, because I get to be with Brian today, because the real Brian is here. And I get to be my best-self as well.
-Gina Patridge
Beloved Wife of the Author

SPECIAL ORDERS!

Want _10 or 1,000+ LP Books_ for a Group or Event?

CONTACT US FOR SPECIAL ORDERS & SPEAKING ENGAGEMENTS!

(Discount schedule available upon request)

info@conebreadpublishing.com

Cone Bread Publishing LLC
PO Box 6674
Aloha, OR 97007

503-567-2939

CONE BREAD
—PUBLISHING—

National Suicide Prevention Lifeline
1-800-273-8255

I've called them more than once; and they saved my life!

~b

Calm And Ground

Common Ground

Come Aground

From Consciousness'

River

And

F.L.Y.

www.ingramcontent.com/pod-product-compliance
Lightning Source LLC
Chambersburg PA
CBHW021216090426

42740CB00006B/250